C000226062

Listen to the Land Speak

A journey into the wisdom of what lies beneath us

Manchán Magan

Gill Books

Gill Books
Hume Avenue
Park West
Dublin 12
www.gillbooks.ie

Gill Books is an imprint of M.H. Gill and Co.

Extracts from 'Bogland' from *Door into the Dark* and 'Strange Fruit' from *North* by Seamus Heaney included with permission of Faber and Faber.

9780717192595

Illustrated by Steve Doogan
Designed by Bartek Janczak
Printed by ScandBook AB, Sweden
This book is typeset in 12 on 17pt, Adobe Garamond Pro

The paper used in this book comes from the wood pulp of sustainably managed forests.

A CIP catalogue record for this book is available from the British Library.

5 4 3

MIX
Paper from
responsible sources
FSC® C021394

Do Chróine, le grá ó chroí, agus buíochas
do shaibhreas na hoidhreachta
a bhronnais orm.

CONTENTS

PREFACE

I woke up one morning in my girlfriend's camper van on a rocky outcrop in Co. Cork with two conflicting thoughts circling through my mind. We were parked up on a stretch of clumped marram grass and sea campions so that when the sun rose we'd be staring straight out onto the Atlantic towards Newfoundland. There were caves and caverns beneath us that had been excavated two thousand years ago by our ancestors, who mined copper here, and over the centuries since then the caves became associated with the deeds of mythical figures from the Iron Age and then with real-life smugglers from the eighteenth century.

The first idea that struck me as I steeled myself for an early-morning swim in the waves lapping just below me was that Ireland is rather unusual in a European context in that the superiority of history over legend was never established, nor was there a clear line drawn between them. The legacy of miners in these caves has blended imperceptibly into the folk-tale figures and sea pirates who occupied them later, creating a unified story.

As a colonised people who had a biased and inaccurate account of our past forced on us by an oppressor, we realised that history could be just as fanciful as legend and that neither was necessarily more accurate than the other. We tended to regard both our history and our geography through a mythological lens, realising that myth could hold certain inalienable truths that we had seen corrupted by the colonising forces of the Church, followed by the Anglo-Normans and then the English.

The second idea that landed in on top of me that morning was that landscape is a mnemonic, an arrangement of natural and physical elements that help us remember things that are often greater than the landscape itself. This is not to say that the geographical features are not vital, but as well as being profound and potent in and of themselves, they are vessels for the history, beliefs and culture of our people, going back thousands of years.

These two ideas have led me, two years later, to this exploration of land and the myths associated with it and to their combined ability to unlock aspects of the living landscape. My intention is to bring you on a journey round Ireland and invite you to consider a different way of viewing our surroundings. This little armchair tour should work just as well whether you're living on the island or have never stepped foot on it. We'll start with some of the principal elements of the landscape – rivers, trees, bogs and mountains – and expand outwards from there to encompass wider and wilder ideas.

Go n-éirí an bóthar leat ('May you have success on your journey').

INTRODUCTION

Ireland was in a molten state 4.8 billion years ago and was covered by an ocean of magma. Some 2.3 billion years later, areas around what is now Co. Donegal were pushed up out of the earth's crust, as were parts of Cos. Mayo, Sligo and Tyrone. This foetal version of the land lay between the equator and the South Pole. Two billion years after that again, the granite uplands of Co. Donegal and Leinster were formed, and parts of Ireland may have been pushed as high as Mount Everest, in a dry desert climate. It continued like that, with intermittent periods of severe weathering and extreme temperatures, until the land was ready for the first creatures, such as the tetrapod, whose tracks are still visible in a layer of slate on Valentia Island from 350 million years ago.

My exploration of myth and the landscape isn't going to concern itself with geology or pre-Jurassic creatures: its focus is on humans and the land, starting with the arrival of the first significant groups of settlers ten thousand years ago as the kilometre-thick layer of ice that covered Ireland melted back into the sea and the land began to slowly rebound to its pre-ice-age height. How relatively recent this was can be seen in the fact that parts of Ireland are still in the process of springing up again, recovering from the weight of the ice sheet built up over 2½ million years of repeated glaciation. Malin Head in Co. Donegal has risen several metres since humans arrived and is still rising by 2 to 3 millimetres every year. The land remembers its compression, just as it remembers so much else.

Our relatively recent arrival on the island can also be gauged by the fact that stories of the first settlers are still quite common in both the oral lore and the written accounts that were taken in the form of dictation by monks a millennium ago from poets and other custodians of the inherited knowledge that the seers and druids had kept alive through the generations. Much of it may be make-believe, but anthropologists are finding increasing evidence that there is truth there too, just as indigenous tales from other cultures are now being found to contain knowledge stretching back tens of thousands of years.

The tales of gods and heroes and their interactions with the settlers can seem complex and long-winded, but know that they are worth the effort of decoding. The knowledge and wisdom they contain is often reassuring and occasionally profound. My task is to try to reveal some of this for you, but I'll need your forbearance.

For those of us who have been reared on simplistic narratives and linear timelines, the absence of a reasoned sequence of cause and effect can be bewildering. Modern historical accounts make for a neat story and an easy way to digest reality, but they are not complete. They are an arrangement of carefully selected facts and subjective interpretations made to fit tidily into each other. Think of them as a handy and practical façade, but don't be hoodwinked into believing that they represent anything more than that.

Myths aren't a complete account either, of course, but as a form of interface with existence, they are closer to the truth than the limited, holographic-like presentation we in the West content ourselves with. On our journey through myth and landscape, you'll find yourself entering a maze in which physical reality warps and winds back on itself, with different themes and locations melding and dividing, seemingly on a whim.

The profoundly fractal nature of the Irish landscape will become clear. Any site, no matter how small or seemingly insignificant, can expand to encompass much more than you might first imagine. Modest sites can suddenly open out like the folds on an infinity-scale map, with each acre containing multitudes, including a vast wealth of lore, history, culture and insights just waiting to be explored. Think of Ireland as being akin to how astrophysicists describe space: a realm that stretches on indefinitely, and is endlessly expanding, until eventually it encounters a worm hole that returns it right back to where it started.

*

It is no coincidence that there are hardly any places in Ireland where you are not in close proximity to a site associated with a particular deity or hero and the stories connected with them. The reach of folklore is more extensive than broadband or mobile phone coverage in many parts. It forms a carefully constructed web of stories whose aim is to communicate old knowledge to future generations.

Our ancestors seemed determined to pass on their wisdom to us across time. Nowhere is this more evident than at the ceremonial ritual site of Newgrange on the banks of the River Boyne in Co. Meath. At dawn each year on the winter solstice, one of the most remarkable astronomical rituals takes place there. The rising sun enters an underground ceremonial passage and shoots down into a womb-like chamber beneath the earth, sending its light and heat into the soil and illuminating symbols that are attempting to communicate ideas and concepts to us that we no longer fully understand. It was conceived of and constructed by our Neolithic forebears over five thousand years ago and, having been renovated in the 1960s, it once again operates as it was originally designed. On the shortest day of each year the sun slides down a subterranean passage.

My aspiration is to do something similar: to send shards of light across the landscape, illuminating certain features and patterns, as well as old beliefs and customs that are still in people's memories today and are encoded in the lore and in the environment.

My last book was about language, which is the very opposite of land, in being completely dependent on humans. Without our minds and our bodies, it doesn't exist. It has no life beyond that which we humans bestow on it. Yet the land has always existed. It just is. It needs no help from us. In every speck of its being it is fully present, fully manifested. The choice is ours whether we wish to engage with it in a meaningful way or merely accept it as a backdrop to our lives. From the land's point of view, our choice is irrelevant; but to us, from a psychological, spiritual and physical health standpoint, it can make all the difference.

Please don't be put off by the scattering of Old Irish words, first names, place names and mythological subplots in this book – each is like a mantra, in that it contains within it resonances and reverberations beyond itself, but none of them are really vital to existence. You're free to skip over any or all of them if you prefer.

My primary focus is on finding ways to reconnect with the solace and power that the land has always offered its people by using folklore, archaeology, language, history and careful observation to pick apart the layers of human and non-human imagining that have built up over time in the land. My hope is that we can use these insights to better understand the instincts and outlooks that still inform the Irish psyche today, and maybe even to develop more appropriate ways of engaging with the earth in general and, in particular, with this patch of rocky green ground that has nurtured and sustained our people since we first arrived here.

It's a lofty ambition and I may not fully achieve it, but I hope that together we'll be able to summon up various sites, or elements in the landscape, in ways that allow us to see them in a fresh perspective, so that we may inhabit them deeply and feel sustained by them. My aim is to stir things up within you so that we can all better feel the feelings, sense the senses, and use this land that has nourished its people for so long to guide us back to who we are and where we can go from here.

RIVERS AS GODDESSES

O n a recent journey to north-west Co. Donegal
to gather Irish words about the sea and coastal
practices, I met a fisherman and local authority official,
Donnchadh Ó Baoill, who pointed out a bridge to me
over the Crolly River and told me that its name was
Droichead an Chaorthainn (Rowan Bridge). I noticed a
line of rowan trees growing along the bank, and he said,
'The rowan kept the evil spirits, the wee people, away.
The trees protected the community, because the river was
a dangerous place.'

I presumed he was referring to the risk of flooding, but he went on to say that his grandmother used to warn him not to get too near the river's edge or to approach a lakeside at night, because the fairies passed along these waters in long, shallow boats in search of human souls to take to their realm. If you got too close, they would grab you and pull you in.

The idea of rivers being dangerous has waned in recent years as many of them have now been so comprehensively banked and bridged that their ability to create and destroy, to nourish life and to take it, seems diminished. This was not always the case. Streams and small rivulets were regarded simply as watercourses running through the countryside, but a river of any reasonable girth or length was likely to be more than it seemed. Often they were boundaries between this world and the Otherworld, or else goddesses in their own right.

Ó Baoill told me that the Crolly River had a *dobharchú*, a giant otter, associated with it, which swam the river at dusk looking for young children to take back to the Otherworld, as it was known that the fairies couldn't have children of their own and so needed to steal human ones.

This concept of water spirits taking children is a universal one. Throughout Africa and South America there are tales of sinister beings who drag unaccompanied children into their watery realms. Greece and

Mexico have similar mythical water characters who lurk along riverbanks grieving their own lost children and waiting for human children who wander by. Estonia also has a female water deity who is cunning and can beguile passers-by with her seductive voice that resembles the hypnotic murmur of a river.

In Ireland, stories about such things were told around the fire to whoever was gathered in for a night's *bothántaíocht* (the practice of frequenting neighbours' houses to hear old stories), and so children learnt to accept them as part of their reality, questioning them only later, if ever. Such stories played a central role in protecting and guiding the community.

The notion that rivers were boundaries and that one could be sucked across into other realms through them certainly lent them potency. It changes one's view of a river to believe it has autonomy and even internal desires. If a river did succeed in capturing a soul to offer to the underworld, you could ask it to show you where it had discarded the empty body. I remember as a child in West Kerry hearing news on the radio of a young boy who was believed to have drowned in the River Boyne at Slane in Co. Meath. An elderly neighbour who was in visiting my grandmother suggested that they should light a candle and place it in a little jar on top of the last sheaf of wheat gathered in the field at harvest time and then send this floating down the river at night. He swore that it would lead the searchers downriver to wherever the body had been caught up in the bank or the reeds.

Folklore is full of tales of rivers working in conjunction with good kings and chiefs to help feed people by bringing fertility to the soil and water to the crops. In contrast, a bad king (an unjust, unwise or infertile one) would alienate the river, and the land would suffer as a result. Rivers would often conspire to protect those who showed deference to them – flooding a ford as their enemies approached, for example, or washing away a bridge to stop an army advancing. There are even accounts of them rising up and drowning whole battalions, then sweeping them out to sea.

This idea is based on the ancient concept of sacral kingship, in which the king was wedded to the sovereign deity of nature, ruling only with the support of its grace and power. Legends recount stories of kings performing rituals that suggest a carnal relationship between the king and the land, and phallic-shaped stones are found at ritual or coronation sites. This idea was alluded to regularly in poetry up to the eighteenth century. Poets described rivers teeming with fish as a result of the power and fertility of the local chief.

We've all experienced rivers communicating with us, soothing our frazzled thoughts in those moments when we gravitate instinctively towards them with harried minds, or inspiring a moment of heart expansion as we catch a glimpse of shimmering beauty while driving over a bridge, or invariably sparking floods of warm elation in us when we dare to go for a quick summer's dip.

The Iron Age myth of Táin Bó Cuailnge is in many ways a paean to the power of rivers – their prophetic ability, their life-giving ability and their destructive or protective ability. The Cronn River in Co. Louth defended the people of Ulster by flooding the valley of Glenmore to slow down the advance of Queen Maeve's Connacht army, and later on Cú Chulainn summoned two other rivers to flood, the Glas Gatlaig and Colpa, and they drowned the enemies of Ulster and washed them out to sea.

Today these rivers seem inanimate and unremarkable, but that may be simply because we've forgotten how to see them fully and to communicate with them. If you are ever on the Cooley Peninsula in Co. Louth, it's worth stopping on the main road to Carlingford at the Cooley Distillery and looking to the north, where you'll see the Cronn (now known as the Big River), which loops around the distillery and continues up through the valley of Glenmore that separates the two ridges of the Cooley Mountains. You can imagine Queen Maeve's foot soldiers and charioteers marching from the west and being suddenly stopped in their tracks by a flood that had been summoned at the ford here.

Likewise, when you're driving to Belfast along the

M1, look to the east just past Dundalk and you'll see the Flurry River, which was known as the Glas Gatlaig. Again, it's not hard to summon up from the past an image of the water rising up and sweeping Maeve's war chariots into Dundalk Harbour. The name Glas Gatlaig derives from the word *glas*, which means a lock or a fetter or a stream, and *gatlaig*, which is a withe or a fastening made of willow. It is explained in Táin Bó Cuailnge that the name derives from the practice of people swimming their cattle and sheep across the river using ropes and willow rods to stop them being swept away, and then just discarding the ropes and sally rods in a heap there.

This idea of rivers purposely harming humans was still being invoked into the late nineteenth century. In 1887 the Scottish newspaper *Highlander* reported that two rivers in Uig on the Isle of Skye broke their banks and flooded in the direction of the lodge of a heartless estate factor of the cruel landlord, Captain Fraser. Not only had the waters risen against him but so too had the dead, who were unearthed from their graves and washed up by his house.

There's no doubt that rivers were considered to have an elemental power and that they contained access to wisdom too. The tenth-century text Immacallam in Dá Thuarad ('Colloquy of the two Sages'), for instance, states that 'the bank of a body of water was a place where knowledge was always revealed for poets'.

Some of this belief seems to extend back to the Indo-European roots that we share with the Hindu culture in India. The name of Ireland's most significant mythical river, the Boyne, shares a linguistic root with the Hindu god, Govinda (an epithet of Krishna), as the Boyne was considered a manifestation of the goddess Boann, which derives from *bó fhionn* (the white, radiant, or clear-seeing cow). *Bó* is the Irish for cow, and *go* is the Sanskrit. They come from the same root. The 'vinda' in Govinda comes from the Sanskrit *uind* (to find out or know), which is related to this same early Celtic word, *vindos* ('white' or 'light' or 'clarity', as in the notion of being able to see through the veil to what lies beyond). Govinda and *bó fhionn* are practically the same word.

The divine cow is a symbol of how rivers, like cows, nourish people with their life-giving liquid, which is why in Ireland you'll find rivers named after the cow. The reference to the cow was a reference to the goddess. The Irish name of the Boyle River in Co. Roscommon, An Bhúill, may come from the Old Irish *búaib* ('cow') or *búaball* ('ox'), and Bó Guaire ('Guaire's cow') is the old name of the River Blackwater in Co. Meath.

And as if to make it clear that these names refer to the cow not as a farm animal but as a symbol of the goddess, the river from which the king of Ulster was forbidden to drink during daylight, according to legend, was known as Bó Nemid ('sacred cow').

THE RIVER BANN

The divine aspect of rivers is not confined to their being referred to in a symbolic way as cows. Often they were named directly after a known goddess. The River Bann, for example, in modern Irish is An Bhanna, which derives from the earlier Banda, which the scholar T.F. O'Rahilly claimed derives from *ban* and *dea*, meaning 'goddess'. Likewise, the Bann in Co. Wexford and the Bandon in Co. Cork are also derived from the name Banda.

There is much to unpack in the mythological and psychogeographical significance of the River Bann, which rises in the lore-rich region of the Mourne Mountains in Co. Down, where the mythic Fianna warriors used to hunt for wild boar and deer and where the nature deity Cailleach Bhéarra sheltered underground beneath a vast stone cairn. It's also where the semi-divine hero Cú Chulainn defended Ulster against the armies of Queen Maeve. The Bann flows into the mystical waters of Lough Neagh, which according to legend was created by magic urine from a horse belonging to a god who is often associated with love and youth, Aengus Mac ind Óic.

That last line requires a brief explanation about Eochu, the son of a Munster king who fell in love with his stepmother, Eibhliu. Eochu and his stepmother eloped northwards through Leinster, fleeing from the king, and when they reached the River Boyne they encountered the divine being Aengus, at his home at Newgrange. As well as being a god connected with love and youth, Aengus was also the son of Bóann, the goddess who was said to have created the Boyne by drowning in its source waters. When Aengus learnt of their disloyalty to the king, and their somewhat incestuous relationship, he was outraged and killed their pack horses. But he then realised they were stuck there, with no way of leaving, so he lent them a horse to continue their flight northwards – on the condition that they return the horse when they reached their destination.

Once they got to Ulster they were so relieved to be safe from the king of Munster that they forgot to send Aengus's horse back. This irritated Aengus and so he made his horse begin to pee. Before long, the urine had pooled into a well that just kept rising until Eochu had no option but to put a capstone on top to stop it. All was then well, and this story would have just been about the importance of returning things (and also about the perils of eloping with your stepmother), except that one night Eochu forgot to put the capstone back in place, and the water of what had now become a sacred well kept overflowing until the entire region was covered in sacred pee. It drowned Eochu in its endless ammonia-rich water, and Eibhliu too. Eventually, according to the legend, it formed the giant lake that is now Lough Neagh, the largest lake in Ireland.

The story sounds outlandish, but Prof. Mike Baillie of Queen's University, Belfast, has calculated from ancient specimens of preserved tree rings that the plain of Lough Neagh may have flooded in 2354–45 BC, which ties in closely with an account in the ancient annals – the annual records of historical events that were passed down through oral lore and later written down by monks – that in 2341 BC Maigh Lughaidh (the Plain of Lughadh) was flooded by a spring that helped clear the ground. Maigh Lughaidh is believed to be in the vicinity of Lough Neagh.

An alternative origin story for Lough Neagh claims that the great warrior Fionn mac Cumhaill created it by picking up a large stretch of land and hurling it at a Scottish giant. The missile overshot the giant and continued into the Irish Sea, forming the Isle of Man, and the massive crater left behind became Lough Neagh. This sounds equally outlandish, but Prof. Baillie suggests that the mention of the Isle of Man hints at a deeper meaning, as the island was the dwelling place of Manannán mac Lir, the sea god, whose symbol is a triskele (the triple spiral motif that is often regarded as a sun symbol and is similar to the current triskelion symbol of the Isle of Man).

Triskele shapes in ancient art are interpreted by some anthropologists as representing a comet, and indeed Prof. Baillie believes that some accounts of the gods flying through the sky might in fact be folk memories of passing comets. There's often an uncanny coincidence of the appearance of fiery, flying characters in the old tales and the known dates of comets passing over Ireland. He suggests that in the case of Lough Neagh, its origin story might be a record of a scorching comet tearing through the sky and then crashing down to leave a massive indentation somewhere nearby. He points to the fact that Fionn mac Cumhaill's first name, though often thought to refer to his fair hair, can also be translated as the 'bright one' and that the Isle of Man has an extra association with comets in the form of its symbol and luminous god, Manannán mac Lir and his flying white horses.

Anyway, all of that is a diversion from our description of the River Bann, which passes through the horse-urine waters of Lough Neagh to emerge on the other side as the Lower Bann, which then meanders along the borders of Cos. Antrim and Derry, through what used to be the Irish side of the Kingdom of Dál Riada (a realm that extended across the North Channel to include part of the Inner Hebrides and Argyll in Scotland). The Bann flows on for sixty kilometres until it reaches the Atlantic Ocean at an area that was known as Inbhear Tuaighe but is now more commonly called Magilligan Strand, a ten-kilometre stretch of sandy beach that is the largest accumulation of coastal sands in Ireland.

This vast expanse of tiny quartz shards and pulverised shells was created by the retreating ice at the end of the last ice age. The sea level began to rise as the climate warmed and as glacial meltwater came gushing down the Lower Bann and River Foyle, bringing with it boulder clay and other eroded material, which eventually formed into gravel ridges around which the sands were deposited.

Just offshore, a sand shoal known as the Tuns Bank, created by the melting ice, protects the strand and has caused many ships to founder. This name may be connected with the Tonn Tuaithe, which translates as the 'wave of Tuatha', and it is here at the Tuns Bank that the mythical Tonn Tuaithe resides – a supernatural wave that is one of the three great waves of Ireland, which according to legend defend the island and, on stormy nights, call out to warn of impending threat or attack.

These three waves are sea waves but also sound waves and vibrational waves. Geographers speculate that they may be connected with inland access corridors or ancient ore trading routes or may possibly even be ancestral memories of the postglacial floodwaters that inundated the land when our ancestors first arrived on this island. This is given further credence by the folk stories that claim that a storm god of Tuatha Dé Danann is buried on the Tuns Bank. Over the millennia this storm god became equated with the sea god, Manannán mac Lir, and still today on stormy nights with rough seas people will hear the call of Tonn Tuaithe and remark that 'Manannán is angry.'

The storm god is also equated with Tuag of Tara, who is said to have died here, and she too is buried on the bank. In fact, the region is known as Inbhear Tuaighe in her memory. According to the old stories, she was an exceptionally beautiful and happy child who was orphaned young and became the obsessive love interest of the high king of Ireland, Conaire Mór, who was determined to marry her when she came of age. This king, who, it is said, reigned two thousand years ago, sent a druidic harpist with magical powers, Fer-Fi (Feardhia in some accounts), from the Upper Bann, to entrance her foster family with one of his softest and sweetest lullabies so that he could then steal young Tuag from her cradle and carry her back to Conaire Mór's royal fort.

The king gave little Tuag to his female attendants to care for until she was ten years old, at which point she was sent to Fer-Fi's fort on the banks of the Upper Bann to learn music and gain a literary education. As she grew, rumours spread of her intelligence and musical ability, and this, allied with people's awareness of her beauty, meant that every prince in Ireland yearned to woo her. Yet none dared to go up against Conaire Mór, until eventually Manannán, who ruled the Isle of Man, heard about her and decided to marry her. He bribed Fer-Fi to bring her as far as the mouth of the Lower Bann to the coastal region where his great powers began and Conaire Mór's waned.

Fer-Fi had a boat hollowed out from the trunk of a giant oak that grew on the riverbank, and once all the preparations were made, he put his young student to sleep again using his magical harp and carried her into the boat. They glided down the River Bann, past the thickets of hazel and willow and soaring stands of oak that rose on each side, until they reached Lough Neagh, where Fer-Fi erected a mast and sailed the giant canoe across the lake to the Lower Bann while Tuag slept peacefully inside. From there, the river brought them through the broad valleys of the kingdom of Dál Riada until finally they reached the sea.

This should have been the end of the story, but unfortunately Manannán wasn't waiting for them, nor was the fleet of otherworldly ships that Fer-Fi had hoped to find. In fact, there was no one there and Fer-Fi panicked. He felt sure that Conaire Mór's soldiers would be in pursuit and would torture and kill him as soon as they reached him. Tuag was still asleep and he couldn't decide what to do. Eventually, he decided to lay her down on the Tuns Bank while he went off in search of another boat to take them both across to the Isle of Man.

But as soon as this powerful harpist seer had gone, Tuag was no longer under his protection, and a great wave rose up from the sea and swept in over the bank. It drowned her instantly because she was still sleeping and so couldn't flee. A storm then rose up and killed Fer-Fi too. When news of Tuag's death reached Conaire Mór and his subjects, they wailed in anguish, and a decision was made to change the name of the place from Inbhear Glas ('green rivermouth') to Inbhear Tuaighe ('Tuag's rivermouth') in her honour. It still bears that name today, though few now use it.

The wave that killed Tuag, Tonn Tuaithe, was one of the three great supernatural waves of Ireland, which are potentially folk memories of the floodwaters that were washing off the land as the ice sheet was retreating northwards ten thousand years ago. They are described in the Dinnseanchas – a collection of ancient legends connected with the lore of notable places passed down by word of mouth before being written down by monks in the Middle

Ages – as the 'three waves of all Erin: the Wave of Clíodhna, the Wave of Rudraige, [and] the Wave that drowned Mac Lir's mate, that visits the shore by Tuag Inbir.'

These supernatural waves are still with us today. Cathal Ó Baoill from Newcastle, Co. Down, has assured me that neighbours in his area know Tonn Rudraige (Ruraí) as the tidal bore between Dundrum Inner Bay, at the town of Dundrum and Dundrum Bay, which is part of the Irish Sea. 'When the tide is coming in, there is a strong current from the outer to the inner bay,' he explained to me, 'and when the tide is on the ebb there is a strong current heading to the open sea.' Until recently there was a pub in the Main Street of Dundrum called Tonn Rory. Every year, Newcastle Yacht Club holds a picnic in the Inner Bay, and it is timed so that the yachts come in and out with the changing tide, using Tonn Rudraige to propel them.

Tonn Clíodhna, at the mouth of Glandore Harbour in Co. Cork, is believed locally to have been involved in the sinking of the trawler *Tit Bonhomme* in January 2012, which caused the death of five of its six crew members. The Marine Casualty Investigation Board judged that the shipwreck was caused by fatigue among the crew and inadequate watch-keeping arrangements, but the fact that it was less than two kilometres from the port of Union Hall, in an area that the captain and crew were familiar with, made local people wonder whether the goddess Clíodhna had come out of her hiding place beneath the rocks of Glandore Harbour to cause ructions in the human world once again.

Before we move away from the story of Tuag and Conaire Mór, it's worth noting its similarity to a story from Hindu culture that appears in one of the ancient epics of India, the Mahābhārata. It's the famous tale of Sakuntala, who was the foster child of the hermit Kanya. When she was discovered in the forest of King Dusyanta, the king determined to make her his wife. They gave birth to Bhārata, who was an ancestor of the Kauravas and Pandavas, two rival groups of cousins whose endless conflict is a central theme of the Mahābhārata.

The story doesn't correspond exactly to that of Tuag and Conaire Mór, but it is a lot closer to an associated Irish myth, the Music of Buchet's House. The myth has been preserved in the Lebor Laignech ('The Book of Leinster'), which was written in the twelfth century but contains stories that are far older. It tells of how Buchet retires into the forest with his foster child, Eithne, and of how Cormac finds her by chance and makes her his queen, which leads to all sorts of complications. These parallels and similarities in tales from two distant cultures are no coincidence: the Irish and Indian cultures have many clear echoes between them – resonances that remain from when we were all connected with a central Indo-European culture that migrated out in all directions.

SLIPPING THROUGH
THE DIMENSIONS

What should one do with stories like the one about the beautiful young Tuag being lusted after by two old deities, leading to the destruction of her and her guardian, or the tale of Eochu sleeping with his stepmother and inadvertently creating Lough Neagh? Certainly, they can provide life lessons and moral guidance, but there are more practical ways of learning such things than in long-winded, fanciful stories.

What they do still offer us today, though, is a way of experiencing the land vicariously through outlandish characters, at a time before it had been moulded entirely to our wishes. The Lower Bann is now canalised by the introduction of five navigation locks and gates that control its levels and that are operated automatically from central hubs at Portna and Coleraine. The Bann is still a great source of trout and salmon and has some idyllic stretches of densely forested banks, but its former wildness has been corralled and controlled. The stories can lead us back through time and help to enchant our view of the river once more.

The Lower Bann is, after all, a remarkably evocative place. The discovery in the nineteenth century of a large number of chipped flint axes on its muddy banks led to the argument a century later that this area may be the spot where humans first set foot in Ireland. (This has been challenged by the recent discovery of human activity near Doneraile, Co. Cork, from 33,000 years ago, but as archaeologists scramble to catch up with these new findings, the high ridge overlooking the river at Mount Sandel, Co. Derry, remains a site of much speculation.) The unassuming patches of dark charcoal-stained soil that were found there may not sound like much, but they turned out to be the pits, post-holes and hearths of early hunter-gatherers in Ireland. These scant burnt residues and ghost remnants of carboniferous forms have been analysed and now offer a remarkably vivid picture of river life here nine or ten millennia ago.

Just as we need to extract the few strands of truth from a myth, archaeologists had to work back from these few meagre clues left in the soil. They noticed lingering traces of holes that were all on an incline. These holes occurred in wide circles or ovals, and each hole was sloped towards the centre of the shape. It seemed logical to deduce that they were left by tent poles – bendable branches that were stuck into the ground and then bent inwards to be tied at the top in the form of a tepee, which was then clad in thatch or animal hides. Directly below where all the branches would have met was a hearth, which is still discernible in the form of layers of burnt or carbonised organic remains.

It is these hearths that offer us the sharpest image of life long ago, as excavators were able to extract traces of what had been burnt in them: fish bones, primarily, mainly salmon and trout, but with some eel too, and a few sea bass.

If you stand there, on a mound that was built over-looking this site during the Norman era, it's not hard to imagine the skin-clad wigwams in the clearings between trees. Beneath your feet are the residues of wooden racks, which would have had fillets of trout and salmon tied to them drying in the breeze or being smoked over a fire for winter storage. The site would have been busy, with people clambering up and down the steep bank to the water's edge, where those first chipped flint axes were found.

In spring and summer these Mesolithic people would have caught salmon and trout heading upstream, while in autumn and early winter eels were trapped heading downstream. When I was last there, in that forest of oak and beech trees clinging onto the riversides, I pulled out my phone and found images of fishing traps that have been discovered from this time. These were ingenious and intricate devices fashioned out of wattle panels, or wicker baskets that had been perfectly preserved in the oxygen-depleted mud of estuaries. The specificity of these glimpses from thousands of years ago made it easier to imagine the adventures of Tuag a mere two thousand years ago, as she made her sleepy journey in the dugout canoe along the Lower Bann.

All around me were hazel bushes beneath and between the more mature trees, and I wondered if they might be descendants of the bushes the tepee-dwellers foraged, as large quantities of hazelnut shells were found in the hearths and middens. It's ironic that the things they purposely tried to discard and destroy are those that have endured, as the carbonisation process preserved them, while the unburnt things dissolved away in the slightly acidic soil. I had read that water lily and crab apple seeds were found too, and in my mind's eye I painted those into the picture, further melding the two eras.

Yet what helps me most to bridge the divide between now and then is the stone tools that were found here

– the small pick-like devices, elongated triangle blades, broad-edged adzes, chopping tools and an array of small geometrical microliths that would have been used in composite tools as knife-edges, barbs and so forth. Holding even replicas of these in your hand is a potent experience. Not only is it a tangible link through time to these people, but it seems to spark a body memory. Your skin, your muscles, your corporeal being recognises something – a distant knowing is triggered.

I was also startled when I learnt of the absence of something that I presumed would be present: bones. No bones from large grazing animals have been unearthed at the site or in fact anywhere in Ireland from this time. Deer bones, in particular, are the one thing you'd expect to find in any significant Stone Age settlement, but they're not present. The only bones of any description found at Mount Sandel were three hare bones, a single dog bone and the bones of some wild piglets that appear to have been born in the early spring. These remains had been discarded in a heap of hazelnut shells that had probably been gathered the previous autumn. The basis of the diet appears to have been largely fish and foraged berries, with the odd duck and pigeon.

Ireland, even then, was very different from the rest of Europe. While deer and the hunter-gatherers who depended on them had roamed throughout continental Europe and even parts of Britain for many thousands of years by then, Ireland was an empty wilderness. It took another seven thousand years for the first deer remains to appear here. And so the pioneering adventurers who settled along the Bann were having to adapt to a more hostile environment, with far fewer species of flora and fauna than they were used to. Palaeobiologists and archaeologists have evidence of at most ten indigenous mammals and a few freshwater fish species at the time the first settlers arrived. A settlement like Mount Sandel might have been able to sustain only a dozen or so people. And even they seem to have struggled, as by 6,000 BC the site was abandoned. This paucity of food was a key factor in why Britain was inhabited for thirty thousand years before anyone even thought of venturing across the channel to Ireland.

And it goes some way to explaining how explorers had made it the whole way across to North America before anyone decided that it was worthwhile crossing the Channel from Cornwall to Co. Wexford, or from Wales to Co. Wicklow, or from what later became the kingdom of Dál Riada in Scotland to the outposts of that same kingdom in the north-east of Ireland.

It should be noted, however, that our understanding of the early settlement of Ireland has been thrown into question by the recent radiocarbon dating of a reindeer bone found in a cave near Doneraile, Co. Cork, a century ago. The bone appears to have been notched with a flint tool and dates back to 33,000 years ago, when Ireland was thought to be covered under a thick layer of ice. It's too early to fully contextualise this new piece of evidence, and so I'm relying on the archaeological consensus that existed up to its discovery, as most other findings of early human settlement are from 9,000 or 10,000 years ago.

Though it was only ever a short distance on calm seas, this bleak, animal-scarce island of ours doesn't seem to have had much to attract the expansive, development-focused mind of a pioneer. Ireland was *in finibus terrae* – at the ends of the earth. Back then it was, as it was still in the early years of Christianity, when St Matthew and the writers of the Acts of the Apostles hinted that Jesus Christ would return once the message of God's love had been spread throughout even the remotest outpost of the Roman Empire and to the very ends of the earth. Matthew was specific on this point: 'And this gospel of the kingdom will be proclaimed throughout the whole world as a testimony to all nations, and then the end will come.' The early hermits arrived in Ireland in the fifth century, and possibly long before then, precisely because they regarded Ireland as the very edge of the known world.

The brave expeditioners who settled along the Bann began to notice over generations that the ice sheet that had covered the land was retreating northwards and that Ireland was beginning to come out of the cold. Because

Ireland is an island, there was no easy route for flora and fauna to recolonise this new expanse of blank earth. Seeds and insects had to blow across on the wind or float across on the waves, or take advantage of land bridges between Britain and Ireland.

On a quiet morning on the estuary of Inbhear Tuaighe, I could almost feel the anguish of Fer-Fi when he realised that the sea god wasn't anchored there waiting and that his precious charge, Tuag, was now in mortal danger. Such is the way that myths are formulated: they get under your skin and linger. But so too do the archaeological finds at Mount Sandel, albeit in a different way. I can sense the concerns of these Mesolithic foragers as they wondered how to carry a clubbed seal upriver and then up the steep valley tracks to their forest camp.

It's an experience rich in resonance. The landscape seems to come more alive, or at least to be discernible from a different point of view. And I've found that any time I've rented a kayak or Canadian canoe and taken to the Bann or Lough Neagh, the intervening eons fade away as my imagination takes root in the timeless nature that still endures here.

THE SHANNON

The very notion of the Bann or any other river in Ireland having potency or being able to communicate with me would have been risible for much of my life. I could easily conceive of such ideas for the great rivers of the world, such as the Ganges or the Amazon, but I regarded the Irish landscape as a mere insignificance, as so many citizens of post-colonial nations tend to do about their home place. At just 0.016 per cent of the earth's surface, this island was merely a speck in the eastern swathe of the North Atlantic that would be dismissed as statistically irrelevant – an extraneous variable – in many fields of science.

Consequently, I had turned my attention away from the parochiality and petty politics of Ireland to explore wider realms – specifically the lands and traditional cultures of China, South America and the Middle East. My twenties and thirties were spent travelling in remote regions of these places, making documentaries about indigenous cultures that were attempting to grapple with the modern world, and I wrote books about my time living in India, Africa and South America.

Only after I had returned home and bought land bordering a stream that was a source for the mighty River Boyne did my attitude begin to shift. The stream began in Lough Lene, which lay a mere two fields to the west of me, and the lake had underground watercourses linking it to Lough Derravaragh, whose waters fed the Shannon. Thus, the two mightiest rivers in Ireland, one leading into the Atlantic and the other into the Irish Sea, were directly connected to the tiny rivulet outside my house. It became apparent to me how everything is connected, whether we see it or not.

The limitless states of consciousness and expanded reality that I had sought in South American sweat lodges and Himalayan caves were to be found here at home too, I realised – and much more besides. I came to appreciate how this small patch of windswept, wave-washed rock can somehow concertina itself, extending backwards and forwards through space and time, so that it encompasses far more than one could ever imagine. There are vast realms of experience, consciousness and wisdom contained within the land and its river systems. Just as a fractal can be limited to a finite area and yet is infinitely magnifiable, so too is Ireland host to an infinity of wisdom and wonder.

Nowhere is this clearer than on the River Shannon, which is as much a multidimensional entity as it is a water source. We've touched on how the River Boyne was considered a manifestation of the goddess Bóann, but the Shannon is on another level entirely, so that it's hard to convey its true essence. I could describe it simply as the longest river in Ireland, stretching from the northernmost tip of Co. Cavan in the north-west through eleven counties and the very heart of Ireland before washing out to sea between Kerry Head and Loop Head in the south-west.

It is 360km long, although, in truth, a river that becomes an estuary has no end to it. Depending on the tides, the sea water can extend up through a third of its length, and the force of the fresh water in spate can send it far out to sea. Along the course of its journey it subsumes a host of tributary rivers, such as the Boyle, Inny, Suck, Mulkear and Brosna Rivers. It is these support rivers that provide its great flow rate, which is double that of any other Irish river.

Now, that's the easy part of the description. The trickier part is conveying the energetic potency of

Ireland's primary goddess river. We should start with its name, which in Irish is Sionainn. Some have said that it derives from the name of the daughter of Manannán mac Lir and the granddaughter of Lear. Still today *lear* means 'sea', and its genitive form is *lir*. So, this argument suggests that in Irish the sea is named after the god who gave birth to it and who is embodied within it, just as the Shannon is named after the granddaughter of the ocean, and it then embodies this goddess within itself.

That Sionainn is the granddaughter of the ocean is appropriate, as the sea water can extend up past Limerick as far as Ardnacrusha. Sionainn is said to have been an intelligent, gifted and generous character, much like Tuag, but to have lacked self-esteem. She had a yearning to learn more, to acquire wisdom and expand her outlook, in particular to have the creative inspiration and ability to write poetry that could change the world.

There are some echoes here with Tuag's experience, although Tuag was too young to make the decision, and so it was Conaire, the high king, who made it for her by sending her to Fer-Fi for an education.

At the time, the principal way to develop one's inspiration was to embark on a literal, or metaphorical, journey of discovery, much as it is still today when people walk the Appalachian Trail or travel to an ashram in India. For Sionainn, it meant a trip that was arduous and not without risk. She would have to travel deep beneath the ocean to Connla's Well, a supernatural spring that could assist one on the journey to knowledge or enlightenment.

Of course, she was warned against it, but the urge to connect with deeper resources within ourselves and to unleash our full creativity is strong. And so, like any good heroine whose actions we are supposed to be inspired by, she set out across the sea to find the well, which was said to have already given birth to six rivers of intelligence.

The powers of the well emanated from nine hazel trees that grew around it, and although the significance of the six rivers and the nine hazels is lost to us, it's likely to have been profound. Each piece of information in the sparse poetic forms that many of our oldest stories are encased in is laden with inferences and allusions that would have triggered insights in the minds of our forebears. Future scholars may unlock these riddles so that their impact can be unleashed, but for now we must rely on our own intuition to interpret them. We need to turn inwards to gauge whether they spark insights or ideas within us.

What is clear from the old poems and many stories that have arisen from them is that the hazels of Connla's Well give birth to magical hazelnuts that, when dropped into the water, transform it into a cauldron of inspiration. The surface of the well froths with what are described as bubbles of wisdom, a form of mystical enlightenment. If this all sounds a bit like a psychedelic hallucination or mystical rapture, perhaps it's meant to.

Sionainn managed to imbibe some of these frothy bubbles, and immediately her gift of enlightenment and creative ability was granted. She turned to head home, but the well rose up and drowned her instantly, just as the sea captured Tuag when she reached the point of possible freedom.

The nineteenth-century translations of the earliest written accounts of this oral lore from the Dinnseanchas emphasised how Sionainn's downfall was a result of her disobedience, of not being content to accept her lot and wishing to advance above her status. That the clerics and patriarchal antiquarians who made these translations would consciously or unconsciously weave this slant into the story is no surprise. Even after twelve centuries of male-dominated Christian rule there was an instinctive wariness of the feminine, of the old goddess-ruled society. Women needed to be reminded of the fate that awaited them if they demanded too much. There was the feeling that the ever-present threat of a strong-willed woman remained.

There's a possibility that Sionainn wasn't a young girl at all, which would put a different slant on things. T.F. O'Rahilly wrote a century ago that her name derived from Senā, 'the Ancient [Goddess]'. The great contemporary scholar Dáithí Ó hÓgáin thought it might come from Senunā ('the Old Honoured One').

Others have suggested that the name comes from Sean-Áine, *sean* meaning 'old'. To get a sense of just how omnipresent the goddess Áine seems to have been in our culture, think back to our predecessors who, legend says, were known as Tuatha Dé Danann, tribe of the goddess Dana (or Danu or d'Anu, which in Irish means 'of Ana', or 'of Anu', or 'of Áine'). These were the supernatural beings we banished underground to the Otherworld when our ancestors first arrived, according to the mythology.

If the Shannon is indeed connected with the goddess Áine/Anu and her followers, what she represents is almost infinite. Áine was deeply entwined with the fertility of the land, the circularity of the seasons and even the cycles of the moon and the tides that are in thrall to it. (It's not surprising that the tenth-century Sanas Cormaic – 'Cormac's Glossary' – includes a text, 'Dúil Dromma Cetta', that describes Áine as *mater deorum hibernensium*, 'mother of the gods of Ireland'.) In short, Áine played a central role in the seasonal repetition of the fertility cycle, which is also what any great river does, whether it be the Nile, the Ganges or the Shannon.

The Áine connection also links her to the Otherworld, which Tuatha Dé Danann occupy, and to their vast Otherworld complex that stretches beneath mountains, lakes, rivers and oceans and that can be accessed through the portals that exist to our world, through rivers, wells, ring forts, tombs and bodies of open water. She is also linked to all this through her birth out of the supernatural Connla's Well, which is part of the Otherworld.

A problem with this idea of the Shannon being Sean-Áine ('Old Áine') is that her youth is a central element of many of the stories about her. Yet even this isn't necessarily a stumbling block, because female deities such as the *cailleach* often represent all ages of a character, through the understanding that time is not linear but cyclical. The *cailleach* is portrayed as a decrepit, withered representation of winter until, on the eve of Imbolc (1 February), she is transformed into Brigid, the maiden of spring. The old woman and the vibrant young woman are twin aspects of the same energy.

One thing that is clear is that Sionainn was regarded as a goddess, as is apparent in an eighth-century Latin text preserved in the Book of Armagh. The text describes St Patrick and his company crossing the Shannon: 'and they came by the River Shannon, which is called Bandea'. Bandea meant 'goddess'. (In Modern Irish this is *bandia*.)

The trope of a well or river drowning a goddess is quite common in Irish mythology. Ireland's most sacred river, the Boyne, has a similar birth story about the goddess Bóann (in some versions the goddess Neachta) going to the Well of Segais in search of knowledge and being drowned. But to see these stories as tragedies is to misinterpret them: what is being communicated is that the goddess dissolves her divine power in the water, which then gives it to the land in the form of fruitful crops that sustain the life force within us.

Ever since humans first learnt to live in communities along the River Nile during the dry season, when the floodplains offered fertile land for growing food, humanity learnt to depend on, and trust in, the life-giving abilities of rivers and also realised that these same bodies of water could take life and destroy land during the flood season – just like the destructive *cailleach* of winter being one and the same as the life-giving maiden of spring, Brigid.

Ultimately, the Shannon is (or at least was) a goddess. This was just an idea that was taken for granted, not necessarily as fact but as an esoteric allusion that had great resonance to it. And it wasn't just the Shannon, as we've seen: many of the great rivers of Ireland were considered semi-divine, and most of the rivers have feminine names.

In the eighth-century tale 'Tochmarc Emire' ('The Wooing of Emer'), Cú Chulainn describes the River Boyne in the form of parts of the body of the goddess, with one part of the river being her forearm, another her calf, another her neck and another her marrow.

But the most interesting element is not just that rivers were regarded as embodiments of female divinity but that so many of the mythical characters associated with them were women seeking knowledge. Tuag was learning from the great druid harpist Fer-Fi. Bóann and Sionainn sought knowledge from the sacred wells.

In fact, Connla's Well was known as a fount of wisdom and a source of insights from the Otherworld. In the rivers dwelt the Salmon of Knowledge, which was regarded as the source of all wisdom and sacred insight. Some tales say that Sionainn caught and ate this magical fish and that this was how she attained wisdom.

Eating the sacred fish, or eating the *cuil crimaind* (the magical hazelnuts that gave the fish its wisdom), was widely accepted as a metaphor for gaining enlightenment. That is what so many of the old stories are really all about: they are elaborate hints leading us to consider that there may be more to existence than our limited, rational brains would have us believe. So much of mythology is about breaking free from the stranglehold of society and our conditioned mind to embrace wider possibilities.

Just as we often find clarity in the shower, or while swimming or walking by the waterside, these stories are trying to remind us that there is a potency to our rivers and that we should perhaps turn to them when seeking insight and answers. On a superficial level the tales can appear, like Christian parables, to be emphasising control, guilt and duty, but if you dig a little deeper they reveal their true message of how we can expand ourselves – and in the process grow in wisdom, strength and self-expression.

The relevance of these rivers of inspiration for us today is that we're living in an age that is crying out for fresh thinking and new insights. There is a need for discoveries and new possibilities, and it can be heartening to know that there is an ancient source of wisdom that we can access through another world of imagination and creativity. For example, the destructive waves that threaten Tuag, Bóann and Sionainn seem uncannily apt in this era of rising sea levels and climate change.

Environmental scientists in Australia have for some time accepted First Nation stories as evidence of climate change more than thirteen-thousand years ago, but we in Ireland are only beginning to explore whether the floods caused by supernatural waves or peeing horses may hint at ancient climate change events. This is so often the way with myths: they appear to mould themselves with eerie accuracy to one's immediate concerns. Their chameleon-like qualities adapt to changing eras and audiences, and different facets of their wisdom can be decoded at different times.

The story of Sionainn reassures me that, while tough challenges may well lie ahead, there is accessible somewhere within us a well surrounded by nine hazel trees of wisdom that flower and fruit every season of the year. This well can never dry up, and it represents imagination, vision and creativity. It is eternal, and as long as the River Shannon flows we will always be reminded of it.

There is, though, one note of caution to sound: the continued flow of the Shannon is under threat as the Government considers a major infrastructure project to pipe millions of gallons of water 170km across the country to the east coast. It is likely to affect the fragile ecosystem of the river and the many aquatic and non-aquatic forms of life, including migratory birds, insects and rare plants, that depend on it. The sheer might of this river has meant that it hasn't been corralled to the same extent as others, and we need to maintain its freedom.

Too many Irish rivers have been banked, dyked and canalised over the past two centuries for the sake of financial productivity. A phalanx of diggers is sent out every few years to dredge the nation's rivers and streams so that the farmland will remain dry and productive. Our obsession with redirecting watercourses and draining land has had a terrible toll on biodiversity. Now is the time to start blocking drains and dismantling human structures to allow our rivers to remember how to be rivers again. We need to allow them to re-establish their natural relationship with the land for their own good – and ours.

SACRED TREES

In the year 2000, to honour the birth of a new millennium, I planted an oak wood around my home near the shores of Lough Lene in Co. Westmeath. I had bought ten acres of sheep pasture, having become entranced by the fact that it extended over a low drumlin of stony gravel deposited by a retreating glacier twelve thousand years ago. Over the years, I shaped and moulded different parts of it into vegetable beds, an orchard, an apiary, a piggery, a hen pen and two small houses. The first house was made from bales of straw that had been grown in neighbouring fields and plastered with lime and clay from the site itself; the second has a sod roof, using soil from the land.

Now, two decades later, the six acres of tiny saplings have become a dense woodland. I chose oak as it was a native tree that shelters more species of insects and lichen than any other, but I had no idea how significant a presence oak could be in the landscape, or in fact of how any native tree in the Irish mindset is so much more than a tree. The fact that the wisdom of the Shannon comes from the nuts that fall from nine hazel trees gives us a hint at this, but the Irish word that makes this most abundantly clear is *bile* (pronounced bill-eh), which means 'sacred tree', 'monument tree' or 'ancient tree'.

This concept of a tree being sacred was not part of my upbringing, or my Jesuit education, or my university degree, but it is indeed the case that for eons in Ireland tribes and specific territories had their own *bile*, a venerated tree in the landscape that was believed to have potency, or to contain the essence of the local people and the surrounding land. With the arrival of Christianity in the fifth century, this idea became heresy, but it nevertheless continued for many centuries. When a tribe raided enemy land, I like to imagine them bringing a branch of their *bile* along with them, held aloft as a symbol of their power and lineage (just as people carried boughs of green branches with them to Daniel O'Connell's 'monster meetings' in the nineteenth century). Naturally, their opponents would go to great effort to capture this branch from them, as any damage to it would have been seen as inflicting harm on the entire tribe and its territory. It was a predecessor to the battle flag.

One of the greatest victories achievable was the destruction of an enemy's *bile*. It was akin to killing the king, though worse, as a *bile* represented centuries of continuous existence, and the sites at which they grew were often inauguration sites for the passing of sovereignty from one generation to another, over centuries. Old manuscripts record the uprooting of important *bili* (plural of *bile*) by adversaries at the inauguration sites of powerful dynasties.

Such were their significance in the landscape that territories were often named after them, like the townlands of Bellia, Billa and Billy in Cos. Clare, Sligo and Antrim, all of which must once have had a sacred, or at least an ancient, tree within them. Also, there are the townlands and regional sites of Bile Chuas (Ballyhoose), Bile Gasta, Bile Éadaí (Billeady), Maigh Bhile (Moville) and Bile Thulláin (Tullin Tree). In fact, of the more than 60,000 townlands in Ireland, 13,000 are named after trees, with the words *beith* ('birch'), *coll* ('hazel'), *iúr* ('yew'), *sceach* ('hawthorn') and *cuileann* ('holly') being particularly common. The most common of all, though, is *dair* ('oak'), or variations of it, such as *doire* ('oak wood'), *dairbhre* ('oak forest'), *doirín* ('little oak grove') and *dearmhaigh* ('oak plain'). This was because the oak was considered the strongest, longest-lived and most venerable of trees.

The ancient laws of Ireland ranked trees in order of nobility, and the oak was always at the top. It's the most dominant and slowest-growing tree, and it is invaluable for construction, barrel-coopering, boat-building and furniture. Its bark was also used for tanning leather and making black ink and dye. As one of the largest trees in the landscape, it often attracted lightning, which further heightened its allure. The Roman philosopher and writer Pliny the Elder wrote that oak was the most sacred tree for druids and that the root of the word, *dru*, stemmed from an old word for oak. This may not be true, but it seems that many types of tree were venerated by pre-Christian settlers in Ireland.

Roman historians from the first century AD, such as Pliny and Publius Cornelius Tacitus, claimed that people who spoke Celtic languages throughout Europe worshipped at groves of trees (mostly oak) that were considered sacred, called *nemeta* (singular *nemeton*). The word is connected with the Old Irish *nemeid*, meaning 'sacred' or 'venerable', or 'consecrated place'. In Bechbretha, the ancient laws of beekeeping, there are references to *nemed* as a tree that grows on the land of a *nemed*-person (a venerable individual), also a sacred grove, or a tree or grove on Church land.

The elegant pillars that soar upwards towards branch-like arches and then splay out into vaulted roofs in cathedrals strike many of us as being like the tree trunks of a stone forest. Perhaps they were sparked by ancestral memories of the forest groves that our forebears worshipped in. The link from woodland groves to stone churches is still evident in the place names of early Christian sites: St Colm Cille's principal monastic settlement in Ulster is at Derry (from *doire*, 'oak wood'); St Brigid's site is in Co. Kildare (from *Cill Dara*, 'church of the oak'); and St Colm Cille's principal southern monastery is at Durrow (from *darú*, initially *dearmhaigh*, 'oak plain'). All were likely to have been pagan sites of worship in woodland before the first timber chapels and stone churches were built.

So, when we encounter sacred sites of any kind – churches, holy wells, stone circles, monasteries or even mansions built on the site of ancient inauguration sites or regal forts– don't be surprised to see old trees there, the descendants of sacred groves that existed long before whatever archaeological remains survive today.

This is all by way of saying that trees in Ireland are more than sources of firewood, or construction timber, or shelter, or fodder for animals, although they are these things too. Niall Mac Coitir, in his book *Irish Trees: Myths, Legends and Folklore* (2003), notes that native tribes in North America regard the buffalo as sacred,

> since it provides them with food from its meat, clothing and shelter from its hide, and various

implements from its bones. It is seen as a gift from the Creator, imbued with supernatural powers, sacred because of its many important practical uses, not despite them.

It's the same with trees in Ireland: they are both sacred and practical, and oak may have been most sacred because it's the most practical.

Unfortunately, the landscape now lacks many of its old trees and its old-growth forest. Outside St Cynog's Church near Swansea in Wales stands a yew tree that is over five thousand years old. It's only 180km from the Irish coast, and yet it would be unimaginable to find a tree of that age here. Ireland was so exploited by its colonial oppressors that no such specimen could have survived. They felled our forests for shipbuilding, construction and iron smelting. A few venerable trees do still stand proud on the estates of Norman lords who took possession of territories ruled by Irish chiefs, but they are rarely more than a few hundred years old – certainly not thousands.

These few exceptions include the King Oak that sprawls over a vast site just inside the gates of Charleville Castle in Tullamore, Co. Offaly. This imposing giant is like a wise, alien life form that has existed for at least four hundred years, and possibly up to eight hundred. It's definitely worth spending time engaging with if you're ever in Tullamore. You'll be surprised by the effect it has on your mind and body if you open yourself to it.

Thirty kilometres south-west of it is the O'Carroll Oak at Birr Castle, which would have been nourished on the blood of Irish warriors who fought on the castle grounds in the sixteenth century – and also on the soft drinks spilt by present-day tourists. Encountering these remarkable trees is a potent experience, akin to the Hindu practice of *darshan*, in which one experiences the divine or the sublime through contact with a physical object or person.

At one time Ireland would have had many trees as old as the yew at St Cynog's Church in Wales, and some may have been included among the five most sacred trees in Ireland that are often referred to in poetry and folklore. These trees were believed to represent transition points or axial lines between this land and realms beyond. Each had a name and would presumably have had guardians to protect it and to see to its needs, just as a temple or holy well would have today.

To understand this notion fully we need to contend with one of the many myths recorded in the Leabhar Buidhe Leacáin ('Yellow Book of Lecan'), a late-medieval manuscript containing tales, triads and traditional lore from far earlier. It concerns Fintan mac Bóchra, said to have been the oldest man in Ireland, and how he met a giant on the Hill of Tara called Trefuilngid Tre-eochair

('Upholder of the Triple Keys'). In fact, it's worth taking a moment to consider what is being conveyed by this name, which can also be translated as 'Triple Upholder of the Triple Key', or 'Strong Bearer of the Triple Key'. I don't have a definitive answer as to its meaning. One needs to just feel into it and see what one's hunch is, or what intuitions arise.

Fintan described Trefuilngid Tre-eochair as being taller than a forest, with a shining crystal veil on his back and sandals of some mysterious material. In his right hand he carried a branch from which three fruits grew: hazelnuts, apples and acorns. He arrived in Ireland on his way back from a mission to meet the setting sun in the far western sky and was on his way eastwards, to the point of its rising, to find out why the crucifixion of a man in Palestine had made the sun stop shining for a full day.

On hearing this, Fintan and the other seers who were gathered at Tara knew that he was not of their world and must somehow be involved in interstellar matters, yet he also seemed aware of earthly issues. For the people of Tara, their primary concern was how they could possibly feed this giant who had turned up out of the blue and could fit the entire sky beneath his legs; but the giant assured them that his fruiting branch would provide all the sustenance he needed.

The giant then asked Fintan a question that had nothing to do with trees or branches. He asked how the island of Ireland was divided, and Fintan explained to him about the four provinces that still exist today and the extra central one, Mide (modern Mí). It's the characteristics he attributed to each province that are worth noting: 'Knowledge in the west, battle in the north, prosperity in the east, music in the south, and kingship in the centre.' Now, this story was written down in the fourteenth century but is likely to be far older, and yet the characteristics Fintan mentioned are still remarkably accurate today, hundreds, if not thousands, of years later. Trefuilngid Tre-eochair agreed with Fintan's assessment once he'd explained it, and he predicted that these traits would remain for ever. Which they appear to have done.

Trefuilngid then gave Fintan some of the berries and nuts and acorns from his branch and told him to plant them in the parts of Ireland where they would grow best, and it is these that became the five sacred trees of Ireland. They were considered guardians of the five provinces, though there wasn't a tree in each province.

The most important one was planted at the navel of Ireland, at Uisneach, where its roots reached down into the underworld and from where its branches soared up into the heavens, uniting all dimensions through its broad trunk, much as the spine is believed to do in yogic tradition or in sculptural representations of the Celtic deity Cernunnos, a horned god of fertility who is frequently depicted sitting in lotus position with a straight spine that connects the upper realms to the earth.

The three keys of Trefuilngid's name could refer to how the trees that he seeded from hazelnuts, apples and acorns were able to unlock the energies or wisdom or life forces in this world, as well as the ethereal realms above us and the netherworld below – just as every tree interacts with the underland, the surface land and the sky.

This central tree was known as Bile Uisnigh and was probably an oak, though it could have been an ash. To the south of it at Bealach Múna (Ballaghmoon), on the plain of Maigh Ailbhe in Co. Kildare, was the Eo Múna ('yew of Mugna'), although some accounts claim that it was an oak. It was the only one of the five trees capable of bearing the three fruits of its progenitor: apples, acorns and hazelnuts. It produced three crops of each annually.

The third sacred tree was the Eo Rossa, which grew by the River Barrow at Old Leighlin, Co. Carlow, and was also mostly described as a yew but occasionally as an oak. When it was felled, in the seventh century, St Molaise was said to have distributed its timber among the Irish saints, which was probably just an attempt to Christianise an important pagan symbol. Further along the River Barrow, at the monastic site of St Mullins, is an oratory of uncertain date that was allegedly roofed with rafters from the sacred tree.

The final two trees were ash. Craobh Dháithí stood at Farbill, Co. Westmeath, and Bile Tortan was at Ard

Breccan near Navan, Co. Meath. The latter was so big that it was said to be able to shelter all the people of the region beneath its branches during times of danger, though it may not have been quite as big as Eo Múna, which, according to a poem in the Dinnseanchas, could shelter 3,040 people.

HAZEL

While the sacred trees were all considered the most noble species (oak, ash, yew), the most magical and powerful tree of all was something far humbler: the hazel, which can be considered more a bush than a tree. Hazels facilitated access to magic, and none were more potent than the nine hazel trees that grow around Connla's Well in the Otherworld and that are described as *cuill crinmoind aiusa* ('hazels of the science of poetry'). As we've seen, this well is the source of many of the sacred river goddesses that flow through the land, and its power arises from the hazelnuts. At least six *srotha éicsi* ('streams of wisdom') spring from this well, while the well of Segais in Co. Meath gave birth to the wisdom and power of the River Boyne, also through its magical *caill crinmon* ('hazels of composition').

You'll remember that the creation of these rivers arises from hazelnuts falling into the well and then being eaten by salmon, whose bellies become stained by the hazel juices. The salmon then disperse this wisdom in the form of the rivers they swim through, and they also create the river through the act of swimming in them.

But the name *cuill crinmoind aiusa* is evidence that the nuts of the hazel tree were also considered to be the source of the sacred wisdom of poets – and poets were believed to be the custodians of all sacred knowledge on earth. To understand this fully you need to remember that with the coming of Christianity the omnipotent power and wisdom of the druid was taken over by the *filí* ('poets'), as well as by the early saints. These two groups were able to perform supernatural feats and had access to profound wisdom. It's no surprise then that both poets and saints are associated with the trees in various ways.

The poet Niníne felled Eo Múna in the seventh century because a king had refused to grant him a favour. (Other accounts claim that it took a group of poets to accomplish the deed and that Niníne was possibly the last poet who just happened to be the one to make it tumble.)

A similar tale is told about the felling of Eo Rossa in the Life of St Molaise, though it was a group of saints who toppled it. They wanted its timber to make church buildings, but none of them had the courage to wield the axe themselves, so they took turns fasting and praying around the tree, in the hope that the prayers of the most devout would be too much for it to withstand, just as the words of a poet in their prime could kill a person.

The felling of a sacred tree is as likely to be a metaphor for the collapse of the old order as an actual account of the tree's demise, and some tales make it clear that the tree didn't always give up without a fight. When Craobh Dháithí was felled, it managed to kill its near namesake, the poet Dáithí, as it tumbled to the ground. Eo Rossa also appears to have exacted an indirect revenge on St Molaise for killing it. The saint offered some planks from the tree to his neighbour St Moling to roof his oratory with, and when Moling went into the forest to cut extra timbers he was blinded by a piece of woodchip that came flying from the axe.

This link between poets and saints as guardians of sacred wisdom, and also of the sacred trees, could be about linking the five trees back to the original sacred hazel, which was the ultimate source of magical knowledge. So the oak, yew and ash are just bigger, more imposing stand-ins for the truly potent hazel, just as the tiny, humble wren (*dreoilín* in Irish, which derives from *draoi eán*, 'druid bird') is regarded in mythology as being more powerful than the great eagle or hawk.

It's hard to be certain about any of this, but what does seem clear is that trees are often far more than they appear to be. They are central icons of Irish culture, symbolising the nobility of the chief and his relationship with landscape and the forces of nature. They become symbols of everlasting life, which is why you'll find them carved into plaques and crosses, both pagan and Christian, and decorating the margins of illuminated manuscripts.

Even their final act of crashing to the ground is thought to impart wisdom, represented by the direction in which they choose to fall. It was recorded that Eo Múna fell south from Co. Kildare to Co. Carlow, while Eo Rossa fell north-east as far as Co. Fermanagh. Bile Tortan fell south-east to somewhere within Co. Meath, as did Craobh Dháithí.

Bile Uisnigh fell north to what is now Granard, Co. Longford, in the era of the sons of Aed Slane, which was roughly the end of the sixth century and beginning of the seventh. It was a time of the demise of the old pagan order, and the fact that it fell northwards towards darkness and cold hints that this was the destruction of something beautiful that was overtaken by a darker force, Christianity. It may also be significant that it fell to Granard, whose name is derived from *gráin* ('grain'), the suffix *-ard* meaning 'height'.

It fell approximately 32km, according to the lore, while the shortest tree, Eo Múna, fell only 12km. The long median lines they created with their trunks formed part of an interlinking matrix across the island.

RATHCROGHAN

When I returned to Ireland after a decade of travelling in distant lands, I hoped to find somewhere in the landscape that would heal me, or at least help me find more meaning in life. I had spent time with the Tarahumara people in the deep canyons of the Sierra Madre in Mexico and with Buddhist weavers on the barren expanses of the Himalayan plateau of Ladakh. I had lived with indigenous elders in the Ecuadorian rainforest and with members of the Yami tribe on Lanyu Island off Taiwan, who still occupied underground tunnels that offer shelter from typhoons in winter. I'd roamed North Africa with Bedouins and Berbers and sung with the matriarchal tribes of western China. Each culture had provided me with a small piece of the puzzle that I was seeking to put together in my mind, but what I yearned for most was to find some equivalent of the elements and practices that these cultures have, and their profound connection with the land, back here in Ireland.

I had been living permanently in the Irish midlands, east of the Shannon, for almost a decade before I over-heard someone referring to a hidden underground site in the west midlands, across the Shannon, where rites of passage were once practised. Immediately, my ears pricked up. I was on a bar stool in the community hall on Tory Island, off the coast of Co. Donegal, when I heard the woman next to me talking about her work as a water diviner and mentioning in passing that there was a place beneath the ground in Co. Roscommon where the 'sacred realm of the goddess still exists'.

I had seen the woman looking queasy on the boat over from the mainland and she had by then drunk a few pints to settle her stomach, so it was hard to gauge how much credence to give her. She went on to say that it was deep inside a vast, soaring limestone cavern just west of the village of Tulsk, in the centre of Ireland. She had that same naïve, over-enthusiastic expression that I myself occasionally have, which wasn't reassuring.

I was tempted to dismiss the idea, but gradually over the years further rumours about this cavern came to me from different sources. All were rather vague, and no one seemed quite sure whether it was fact or fantasy. I certainly wasn't able to get clear directions to it. But I began to find references in old mythologies to a chamber of transformation beneath the ancient royal capital of Connacht, which lies in that area of Co. Roscommon. So whenever I was heading westwards along the N5 road towards Achill or Ballina, I'd take detours down grassy roads and boreens to see what I could find.

What struck me most was how extensive the so-called 'royal capital' of Rathcroghan was. Wherever I looked I found further standing stones and the grassy humps that signified ring forts and ceremonial earthworks, most of them completely unexplored. There are more than 240 ancient monuments in the area, which puts the site on a par with the great ceremonial sites of Co. Meath, such as Newgrange and Tara, in its cultural importance. Yet none of the detailed excavation and research work that was conducted on the sites of Co. Meath was ever done here, until scientific analysis and LiDAR surveys were carried out in recent years, using laser sensors and other technologies to pinpoint every tiny surface anomaly, from the hearth of a cooking-pit to the grand entrance of a ceremonial temple. These revealed an entire network of linear earthworks, burial mounds, ring forts, field boundaries and temple sites just beneath the thin skin of soil and grass.

The most prominent of the Iron Age remains is known locally as Queen Maeve's Fort. It consists of a steep-sided mound just beside the N5. Scientific mapping revealed broad parade ramps leading up to it and enclosures where ceremonial processions of dignitaries, high priests and perhaps even sacred animals may have been led in great public rituals of kingship, or burial, or nature worship, thousands of years ago.

This area was one of the most fertile territories west of the Shannon and so was able to attract and sustain populations better than anywhere else in Connacht over five millennia. Traditional farming practices continued unchanged during this time, so that in many cases the current field boundaries are those that could have been described in the old tales about Queen Maeve and her warriors. It was from Rathcroghan that she and her army set out to steal the finest bull in Ulster, as described in Táin Bó Cuailnge.

I became captivated by how the area had remained unchanged for so long and how little known it now was. Ireland is a small country, and yet so much of its inland regions are largely abandoned and unexplored, particularly the swathes of land west of the River Shannon that are still far from the Atlantic coast.

I continued exploring the back roads of Co. Roscommon on and off over the years without ever coming upon the sacred realm of the goddess, though

I did hear more and more stories in the area about the quasi-divine figure of Queen Maeve, the ultimate sovereignty goddess described as a 'fair-haired wolf queen, whose form was so beautiful that it robbed men of two-thirds of their valour upon seeing her'.

The name Maeve probably means 'she who intoxicates', and she certainly controlled many men, boasting that she 'never had one man without another waiting in his shadow'. And it took thirty men to satisfy her when her favoured partner, Fergus Mac Róich ('Son of Great Horse') wasn't around. When making a deal, she would often throw in an offer to sample her 'friendly thighs', and it was known that any man who wished to be inaugurated as king had to have sexual relations with her to show that she had conferred legitimacy on him.

Many of the region's archaeological sites are connected with Maeve in lore, from the mound of Carn Láma, which contains the hand of her son-in-law Fráech, to the inauguration site of Carnfree, where the rest of Fráech's body lies together with the skulls of some children that Maeve ate unwittingly, as they had been transformed into piglets without her knowledge.

There's also a standing stone known as Maeve's Butter that is said to mark her grave site, and another known as Maeve's Cheese, which together form a pair of entrance posts leading to the principal ceremonial mound. I even learnt about the three trenches she created somewhere east of Athlone with the force of her menstrual flow when she and her army were retreating from Ulster back to Connacht, having lost a series of battles against Cú Chulainn.

But the secret ritual site Oweynagat (Uaimh na gCat), where Maeve was said to keep her treasure and her Otherworldly cattle, evaded me until one summer evening when I was driving home after a full day of meetings in Mayo and decided to veer off down a grass-lined road that led onto a track that eventually led to a dead end with barely room enough to turn the car. It seemed like a suitable metaphor for reaching the end of the trail, and I determined at that moment to abandon the search entirely.

I began the process of manoeuvring gingerly backwards and forwards, trying to extract myself without ending up in a ditch, when suddenly I caught sight of a group of brightly dressed people in the middle of a field. It's hard to convey quite how unusual it was to come upon anyone in these rural expanses, particularly people dressed in expensive outdoor attire and who could only have been tourists. I realised that the one thing that could have brought them here was the cave. My heart began to beat faster.

I jumped out of the car and clambered over the fence, striding purposefully across the field, expecting to find a great orifice leading into a dark abyss – a ritual entranceway into the Otherworld – but there was nothing there. No cave, no cavern, no hole. Not even a slit in a rock. Just a humdrum west-midland field like all the others surrounding it.

I turned back towards the tourists who were lingering by a field wall and they confirmed that they were indeed here for Oweynagat and pointed me towards a grassy bank that formed the northern perimeter of the field. A hawthorn bush grew from its top, and under it, amid a tangle of brambles, nettles and grasses, was a stone with what looked like a foxhole or the entrance to a badger set beneath it.

This was the entrance to the cave, they said, and their guide, a local expert named Mike McCarthy, was still down inside it, somewhere deep beneath the ground. Immediately, I got down on my knees and began to clamber through the opening in the muddy ground. It was pitch dark inside and I was about to crawl in over wet rocks until I stopped myself, suddenly realising that this wasn't the correct way to enter a cave of such spiritual and mythological importance. I would need to do it properly with suitable preparation and clear intention. I tried turning round to retreat, but there wasn't enough room, so I backed out of the tunnel again and returned to the muddy field, bum first.

OWEYNAGAT

I was anxious to get back to Oweynagat as quickly as I could after that first discovery. What intrigued me most was an account of the cave in the eighth-century tale 'Fled Bricrenn'. It's about a hostel-keeper who invites the three greatest warriors to a feast and offers each the *curadmír* ('champion's portion') of a boar roasting on a spit. All three reach for the most succulent hindquarters, befitting their status as champions, and it leads to uproar as each claims that he is the most deserving. They agree to a series of challenges to settle the dispute, and these extend throughout Ireland over many months until eventually they get to Rathcroghan, where Queen Maeve challenges them to spend a night in Oweynagat with three phantom wildcats, declaring that whoever survives the night will be deserving of the pork. It is from this incident that the cave probably got its name, Uaimh na gCat ('Cave of the Cats'), although it might also have been called Uaimh na gCathanna ('Cave of the Fights').

The men crawl their way into the cave to face the most frightening, torturous and violent night of their lives as Maeve's demonic animals are set upon them. Each man is tested to the very limit of his ability, until at dawn next day the one who emerges victorious is Cú Chulainn.

For me, the importance of this story is that it appears to describe a rite of passage, which is precisely what I had been searching for since returning to Ireland. Up to that point I had no idea that there were any accounts of where these ceremonies actually occurred. The mythology frequently refers to trials that young men had to undergo to enter the nomadic band of Fianna warriors and be accepted by their kin, but the details of what these involved are always scant. This account in 'Fled Bricrenn' appears to provide some sense of the challenges that boys would have undertaken to prove they had reached the age of manhood – albeit with some phantom wildcats thrown in for dramatic effect.

In my years of perpetual travel in my twenties, I yearned to undergo a similar rite – so much so that I travelled high up into the Himalayas to find a suitable cave where I could be alone and embark on a journey of inner discovery to confront the demons of self-doubt and fear and find the endless resources of love and light that I felt must be hiding beyond them. After much searching I had to give up my dream of finding a cave and make do with a cow byre, which I rented from a somewhat bemused farmer in the Himalayan foothills near where India, Nepal and Tibet meet. At first it felt like a setback, but over the following three seasons I got to experience a life-changing, and mostly ecstatic, period of spiritual transformation.

Had I known back then that there were ritualistic caves in Ireland – chambers of transmutation, crucibles for spiritual and psychological exploration – everything could have been different. The more I considered the tale of Fled Bricrenn, the more convinced I became that this was what was being described. Three men descend into the darkness to confront their greatest fears, and only Cú Chulainn emerges successfully, having defeated all the supernatural beasts that the goddess of the Otherworld sends at him.

The original audience of the story would have known that not only were there three wildcats in the cave, but Morrigan, a phantom queen who represented war and destruction, was likely to be there too. She was known to foretell doom or death or to incite warriors to plunge fearlessly into battle. Oweynagat was said to be her dwelling place on earth.

When I first conceived of writing about our connection with the land, I had no idea that any of the ancient natural sites of transformation still existed, as opposed to the archaeological ruins of ceremonial temples with their neat, gravel-lined paths, information boards and ticket booths. I was eager to return to the cave to see how long I could spend within it and what I might experience.

And so a few weeks later I drove back to Rathcroghan and headed towards the hole in the ditch without a phone, torch or other supplies, just an audio recorder to record my thoughts. I sat for a few moments in the field to set an intention for my journey and then posted myself back in through the tiny opening and began clambering along the stone-lined tunnel that led to the actual cave entrance.

I had read that on one of the stones above my head was an inscription written in ogham that translates as '[the stone]of Fráech, son of Méabh', and as I squatted there waiting for my eyes to adjust to the darkness, I wondered whether it had once been a marker pillar on the boundary of land owned by Queen Maeve's son-in-law Fráech. Or did it refer to some other Fráech and Maeve whose names had become common in the area at some later time, based on the local mythology? Or was the inscription a hoax from the medieval age crafted by someone who knew how to carve in ogham script?

After a few metres the ground became wetter and muddier and began descending quite steeply. I edged my way as best as I could over the stones, feeling cold limestone pressing into my shoulders and hips and occasionally banging my head on the rock above. The air grew mustier the further I descended and I could feel the temperature drop.

Soon there was no trace of light left from the entrance, and the sounds of birdsong and the wind through the trees had disappeared. I had entered another realm. I crawled on downwards, heading more or less under the road where my car had got stuck last time and in the direction of Queen Maeve's Fort to the north-east. The sound of my heartbeat grew louder, and it was faster too, as I was exerting energy lowering myself down steep ledges with my arms notched into the cave sides and my feet dangling below me. My voice sounded cramped and dampened, and although I could have been in the cave only a few minutes, I was expending so much energy and maintaining such focus that I soon lost track of time.

I began to think of Morrigan and the way she used to entice men towards their own destruction in battle or elsewhere. Her desire was to whip up chaos and shake us out of complacency and comfort. She certainly had had her way with me: I had not told anyone I was coming here, as I wanted to succumb entirely to the experience, without any safety net or escape strategy. If Maeve was going to send her phantoms, I wanted to fight them off alone.

Once or twice my foot slipped, or my hand failed to grip, and I banged my head quite badly on jagged rocks jutting out from the sides or the roof. At one point a wallop of my head brought on a bout of dizziness and I thought I could feel blood in my hair. I wished I had thought to bring a helmet or allowed myself a torch.

The blood was probably just mud or slime, but as I imagined it oozing slowly from my scalp, I pictured Morrigan in one of her typical poses, washing her hair or clothes in the river only for an observer to realise that the entire river had turned to blood. In the tales, the observer would then realise that she was washing away the spoils of battle and the destruction that she had sparked. She had successfully enticed me down into her lair and I was now at her mercy. I licked the moisture that was oozing down my scalp to check if it was blood, but it tasted more of mud than iron.

The one thing that medieval versions of these prehistoric tales were clear about was that Morrigan hated intruders and was known to let loose dark spirits to terrorise the minds of those who dared trespass in her realm. The thought of it sent a chill running down my spine, and my mind began throwing flashes of phantom light in front of my eyes, though my rational brain knew there was nothing there. It was just that the optic senses were confused at the lack of stimuli and were casting out apparitions in frustration.

I knew I had to keep a hold of reality, to keep the fear and darkness at bay. I began to sing to myself and I was surprised to hear the notes echoing out into a larger space than I had imagined. That was reassuring. It meant I must have reached the cave bottom and I realised I could now stand up and swing my arms around as the limestone fissure had opened into an expansive, soaring space. My chanting sounded as if it was resounding through a lofty auditorium.

Relieved to have finally made it, I squatted down on the ground and settled in for as long as I could endure it. The rock was less muddy here, which offered me some reassurance that the underground river that had carved this cavern through the limestone wouldn't return to drown me, but images of sudden downpours above, causing the whole cave system to flood, still flashed through my mind. I knew the chances of a deluge were slight, and yet my mind latched onto it and also began repeating the words *Dorus iffirn na Hérend* ('Ireland's door to Hell'), which was how the cave was described in the ninth century.

I dismissed all such thoughts as the meddling of Morrigan or Maeve and just tried to clear my mind and sit quietly, breathing and occasionally singing into the abyss. Having my recorder was a great help as talking into it made me feel less alone. My plan was to edit the monologues into an episode of my podcast *The Almanac of Ireland*, and the thought of that helped keep me focused, though it probably also prevented me from experiencing the isolation of the cave to its full extent. It's hard to know how long I stayed down there. It was definitely a few hours, but it wasn't all night, which I had initially hoped for.

I began to think of the mythical warrior Nera, who once came upon Queen Maeve's fort burnt to the ground with all its dignitaries and warriors beheaded. In the story 'Echtra Nerai' ('Adventures of Nera') he is said to have chased the attackers down into this cave, where he came upon the heads of his friends mounted on spikes. The king of the Otherworld, realising that all members of Nera's tribe were now dead, took pity on him and offered him a wife to keep him company and a job fetching firewood for the fairy mound. Nera settled into this new life and was reasonably content until his wife revealed that his vision of the burning of Queen Maeve's fort was actually a premonition of what would happen next Samhain. He realised immediately that he would have to return to the real world to warn his friends of what was to come.

At some point in the evening I began to feel something similar. There was no premonition of tragedy, just a keen urge to get back to my world and start communicating these ways of engaging with our land and our past to others. I felt I had got as much as I was ready to experience from the cave and began to crawl back up through the tunnel, feeling a wave of elation as I sensed the first wafts of fresh air in my nose and as my eyes began to discern the first glimmers of light from above.

I emerged into the light profoundly grateful that this island has managed to preserve such ancient sites of spiritual transformation. Oweynagat is a potent place, and thanks to the dedication of the local community it is now accessible again. There are no signposts to it, as it is on private land, but anyone who wishes to visit can drop in to Rathcroghan Visitor Centre in the village of Tulsk and book a tour of the site with the incredibly passionate and knowledgeable local guides. It was wrong of me to have gone there without first checking in with the centre, as they have an agreement with the landowner to monitor access to his land. In all subsequent visits I've always dropped in to them first.

TÍR NA NÓG

By now it should be clear that one can't explore the tangible elements of the Irish landscape – its rocks and rivers, trees and towns – in any depth without taking account of what lies beyond. This world and the Otherworld are so intermingled in our consciousness that we cannot consider one without the other. They are conjoined aspects of the same reality. It's just a lot harder to describe and define the spirit world, *An Saol Eile* ('The Other World').

Many would claim that it doesn't exist, or at least not in this plane of existence, but for eons people insisted it lay somewhere to the west, out beyond the Atlantic, along the 'golden way' that extends across the sea as the sun sets. This route is called Mag Mell ('Plain of Honey'), referring to the golden plain that shimmers across the sea before sunset.

Although it is supposed to be some distance away, there are access points on certain lakes, rivers, bogs and waves, or else through caves, burial cairns, fairy forts or even mists. It is said that people occasionally use a magical boat or horse to travel there, but a powerful spell can get you there just as easily. The journey is rarely straightforward: dangers or hurdles must be surpassed, and once you get there, further hostility can await. Alternatively, you can be lured in by a fairy lover or a trickster and find yourself trapped there for prolonged periods that are often multiples of three in duration – three days, three months, three years or three centuries.

The conflicting accounts seem to convey that there is a process, either physical or internal, required – something that would spark a change of consciousness, an altered perspective. There was also a common, but mystifying, belief that if you were attempting to approach the Otherworld, you were already within it, as if the very act of committing yourself to it brought you there, which does make sense in a non-temporal, non-linear world.

Describing the geography of a non-physical dimension is not easy, and yet it's important that we get some sense of it, as aspects of the Otherworld tend to bleed through into our dimension quite frequently.

The realm most referred to was Tír na nÓg, but it's hard to know if this was a single place or a collective term for these other dimensions or planes of existence. Tír na nÓg means 'Land of Youth', although 'na nÓg' is probably better translated as 'of the Ever-Young' because it refers to a world beyond time in which events occur in a non-linear sequence, much like how time was defined by Einstein and Heisenberg in the early twentieth century. Tír na nÓg is the land of youth because, without time, aging is not an issue. Everyone is young, or at least ageless, there.

Other names that could be synonyms for Tír na nÓg, or may represent entirely different realms, are Má Mheallach ('Enticing Plain'), Tír faoi Thoinn ('Land under the Wave'), Teach Doinn ('House of [the fairy lord] Donn'), Inis Subha ('Island of Joy'), Airgtheach ('Silver House' or 'Silver Place'), Eamhain Abhlach ('Twins with an Abundance of Apples') and Má dhá Cheo ('Plain of the Two Mists').

Since these realms don't operate within our conventions of space and time, their appearance seems to change sporadically. Some accounts describe them as consisting of forested wilderness, while others describe flower-clad meadows buzzing with bees. There are tales of cities and fortresses made of precious metals and feather thatch, while other tales home in on a sacred well at the heart of the land, surrounded by a grove of nine hazel trees or a single dominant tree with a bloom on every bough.

One of these trees has an enchanted silver branch laden with golden apples. The well is inhabited by a sacred salmon, and dangling above it is a drinking horn or an enchanted cup. (This sacred cup is reminiscent of a chalice, because, of course, Christianity borrowed most of its central tropes and tenets from previous faiths.)

Things are rarely just one way in the Otherworld: they depend on how they are being perceived and how the observer interprets them, like how quantum physics describes all possibilities as existing simultaneously until the point at which they are observed. In Tír na nÓg, reality is never just one thing: it is 'both', 'and', depending on your outlook and your wishes.

Any attempt at describing these places can therefore capture only a meagre, imperfect shadow of what they truly are. Such multidimensional, all-encompassing realms are better hinted at than described in detail. I can imagine *seanchaithe* ('storytellers') scoffing at my crude definition of such realms here. They would claim that such information cannot be transmitted through text. It needs a group of people huddled around a fireside and a long, dark night, or better still a number of nights. A dark winter. A lifetime.

For each element of Tír na nÓg and its other sister lands there are key concepts that must be communicated. For instance, its sacred well is sometimes regarded as the birthplace of humanity, even of the entirety of existence.

The tree that looms over the well is considered the axis of the world. It is the central tent post of this circus realm we inhabit and also the central tenet on which the druid's power is based. The part of the sacred tree known as the 'silver branch' is a metaphor for a concept that is beyond my ability to communicate – a concept as vast as any ocean. Some accounts claim that the birds living on the tree represent all the souls of the dead.

But we can bypass all this metaphorical vastness by merely understanding that, at heart, what Tír na nÓg and its associated lands represent is the ultimate place of nourishment, nurturing and mind expansion. We can get a better sense of it by turning inwards and breathing deeply rather than by trying to coax our limited brains into conceiving of something that is beyond it. When we pause and try to feel into Tír na nÓg it will probably respond differently, depending on our needs and our outlook at that time.

Maybe it's easier to say what it isn't: a place of judgement or moral rectitude, like the Christian notion of Heaven. It isn't confining, or preordained. Tír na nÓg was always, and presumably still is, a place where we can be creative, grand, fully realised beings – an expansive realm of health, abundance and joy. If that is something we want to have in our lives, we should consider keeping it, even if we do decide to jettison many other aspects of our customs and traditions.

HY BRASAIL

Now that we've established that the Otherworld exists in some capacity, just not in a tangible, physical way, we need to address the one piece of Ireland whose status remains most uncertain. It may be part of this realm or the realm beyond. It's called Hy Brasail and is, it is said, an island off the west coast of Ireland. It has been imagined, discussed, explored, documented and even mapped for millennia, and yet there's a distinct possibility that it doesn't exist – that it's just a figment of our imagination. Since I aim to get to grips with the resonances and reverberations associated with places, and the multidimensional aspects they may acquire, we need to contend with Hy Brasail before proceeding any further.

Since time immemorial it has been discussed in fireside conversations all along the west coast, where people believed they could occasionally see a landmass in the distance to the south-west. During all these centuries, which may have even extended over thousands of years, the island existed in story and in imagination, without any real need to prove its existence beyond the fact that it was a place that boasted a bounty of riches and where wonderful things happened.

All was well until the Age of Reason dawned and the urge to define and delineate our reality became an oppressive compunction. Landmasses had to be documented and mapped in the belief that everything that mattered could be catalogued in ink on paper.

This false assumption is also at the heart of my work here – the notion that the infinitely variable and largely indefinable essence of Ireland can be captured within a few hundred pages. It's farcical, but I choose to ignore that, just as the Genoese cartographer Angelino de Dulceto in 1330 included the notional island of Hy Brasail on a nautical chart he was drawing for Majorcan navigators and merchant seamen. He located it slightly to the south-west of Ireland and gave it the name Insula de Montonis (or Moutonis) sive de Brasaile, meaning something like the 'island of rams that were reddish like the dye from brazil wood' (or whose horns may have resembled brazil wood branches). In a subsequent map, fourteen years later, Angelino described it as having 'a strikingly round form, often divided by a channel'.

Its appearance on a map could be dismissed as a misunderstanding, the folly of an over-zealous cartographer, except that in 1375 one of the finest and most comprehensive maps of the Middle Ages, the great Catalan Atlas, featured it again. Like all the charts and navigational tools of this great age of exploration, this atlas was considered a serious work of science and reason that aimed to eschew past flights of fantasy or whimsy. Hy Brasail had found itself an unquestionable part of the tangible world, and as such it needed to be explored.

In 1480 an expedition was launched by John Jay, a successful merchant from Bristol, but after nine weeks at sea he returned home with nothing. The following year two more ships set out, but they too failed to locate the mystical island. This was no surprise to people in Ireland, who had always known that the island was largely invisible, hiding behind a dense bank of mist that rose briefly only every seven years. Searching for it at the wrong time was like seeking a blackberry in winter.

Yet this type of expansive thinking (or woolly thinking, depending on one's viewpoint) was unacceptable to the great navigators of the Renaissance. The eminent Venetian explorer Giovanni Caboto (John

Cabot), who was the first European to reach North America since the Vikings, decided that he would discover Hy Brasail. He embarked on two expeditions, but both were ill-fated, and his ships were caught in numerous storms and thrown off course. He did, though, manage to discover a new coastline to the north-west on his first expedition. It was presumably Newfoundland or Cape Breton. On his second expedition some of his ships were damaged in a storm and he himself never returned, but it was said that he may have reached Hy Brasail, as in 1497 the Spanish envoy to London described Caboto to the court of King Philip I as having been among 'the men from Bristol who found Brasail'.

The island continued to exist on scientific maps in the sixteenth and seventeenth centuries, and by the late seventeenth century Captain John Nesbit of Killybegs in Co. Donegal claimed to have landed there and explored it. His merchant ship was sailing its habitual route from France to Ireland in 1674 when it got caught in a fog bank and drifted uncomfortably close to a rocky shore. The nautical charts showed they were in the vicinity of Hy Brasail, so they dropped anchor, and Nesbit selected three crewmen to row him ashore. They discovered an island dominated by a stone castle and grazed by domesticated sheep and cattle and with large black rabbits. Some reports claim that by lighting a fire on the shore at night the crew managed to break a spell that destroyed the castle and its tyrannical magician; others claim that old men who spoke an antiquated language bestowed gold and silver on the crew members. The reports were enough for a second ship, captained by Alexander Johnson, to set sail and they too claimed to have found the island and verified Nesbit's claims.

So, the otherworldly island of the mind, which had existed in the collective imagination, or at least beyond the veil of human visibility, was suddenly brought into physical reality, with eyewitness accounts from rational, reasonable men. For several decades in the late seventeenth century it became just another part of the tangible, knowable world, as if an archangel had been embodied in human form.

There were further accounts of first-person encounters with the islanders. The historian Ruairí Ó Flaithbheartaigh in 1684 wrote about meeting a man, Morrough Ó Laoí, who had been abducted by strangers while wandering in a distraught state after an argument with his wife. Two or three men dragged him onto a boat and sailed across to Hy Brasail, where he was held for two days, during which time he became ill. When he recovered he found himself mysteriously returned to Seapoint, near Galway, and at some point later he developed the gift of healing, even though he had never studied medicine.

This story was still being shared in the community almost two hundred years later, in 1846, when the historian James Hardiman published Ó Flaithbheartaigh's account. By then it was claimed that Ó Laoí had been given a book of cures by the islanders. This was most likely a flight of fancy, and yet the book exists today. It's preserved in the Royal Irish Academy (RIA) in Dublin. On the corners of many of its pages are drawings of exotic creatures that don't appear to be from the known world and are probably representations of animals that were believed to exist in Hy Brasail.

We should pause a moment to consider the ramifications of this: in the archive collection of a scholarly institution devoted to scientific research there's a book that's purported to be from beyond the physical realm. Now, believe me, I'm more than comfortable with figments of the imagination and nebulous theories, and after fifteen years of writing for the *Irish Times* I'm not too bad at dealing with the rational, physical world either. But it's the in-between that really throws me. Wouldn't you love to see how the book is categorised and catalogued in the archive's index system?

It reminds me of Nuala Ní Dhomhnaill's claim that the Folklore Commission at University College, Dublin, has a drawer in its index system marked *Neacha neamhbeo agus nithe nach bhfuil ann* ('Non-living beings and things that don't exist'). Occasionally, I hear about the RIA removing the book from its vaults to make it available for public display, and I consider going to see it, but just like I accept that the village of Ballinspittle or the island kingdom of Bahrain exist without needing to set eyes on them, likewise I prefer to accept the possibility of the existence of Hy Brasail and its magical book without needing proof. Perhaps they exist and don't exist at the same time, drifting in and out between our reality and some interdimensional vapour every seven years, like souls incarnating and reincarnating on earth.

One of the last written accounts of Hy Brasail was by the antiquarian and archaeologist T.J. Westropp in 1872. He claims to have seen the island on three separate occasions. On his final visit he brought along family and friends as witnesses.

> It was a clear evening, with a fine golden sunset, when, just as the sun went down, a dark island suddenly appeared far out to sea, but not on the horizon. It had two hills, one wooded; between these, from a low plain, rose towers and curls of smoke. My mother, brother, Ralph Hugh Westropp, and several friends saw it at the same time.

This party claimed that the island had appeared out of nothingness and remained long enough for them all to see it clearly before it vanished beneath the waves again. Even in 1893 W.B. Yeats could write in *The Celtic Twilight* that fishermen along the western seaboard told him they had 'sailed as far as Hy-Brasail', and I've also had fishermen from Connemara in the last few years insist that they've seen the island. There is a great recording from the 1980s of the acclaimed *sean-nós* singer Seosamh Ó hÉanaí recounting his own sighting of Hy Brasail.[†]

What should we do with these claims? Our rational minds will want to dismiss them all as the imaginings of a pre-modern people, and yet everything that science is now telling us points to the fact that the world is a lot more indeterminate and wonder-filled than we ever imagined. It would be wrong to dismiss it out of hand. Certainly, the vice grip of reason had taken such hold by the late nineteenth century that Hy Brasail could no longer be included on maps. Its last appearance was on British Admiralty charts in 1865; but after that there was no longer space in the consciousness of 'enlightened' citizens for the unknown.

Eventually the island suffered from what J.R.R. Tolkien referred to as the rationalisation of the magic world. In 1947 he noted that it had 'become fashionable soon after the great voyages had begun to make the world seem too narrow to hold both men and elves; when the magic land of Hy Breasail in the West had become the mere Brazils, the land of red-dye-wood.'

This pervading doctrine of rational orthodoxy would have us discard Hy Brasail and many of the

† Cartlanna Sheosaimh Uí hÉanaí (Joe Heaney Archive). https://www. joeheaney.org/en/hy-brasail-the-isle-of-the-blest.

more mystical aspects of Ireland as mythical flights of fancy and move on, but that would not only dismiss the central importance of mythical realms but also ignore a deeper truth, namely that Hy Brasail may represent a folk memory of a landmass that did once exist in the area. Just three years before Hy Brasail was last represented on British Admiralty navigational charts, a raised area of the seabed was discovered two hundred kilometres west of Ireland, roughly in the area of Hy Brasail. It's known as the Porcupine Bank and may once have been an island at a time when sea levels were lower. If you study digital maps of the region, you'll see an underwater circular elevation with a semi-circular depression cut through it at the coordinates 52°09'42.5"N 13°13'12.7"W (or at 53°19'59.88"N 13°30'0"W).

Its appearance is remarkably similar to how the island was described in the mythology and represented on charts from the very beginning. The remains of a river delta are visible in the area, and it may have offered an abundance of nourishment to living beings before the deluge caused by melting ice after the last ice age drowned it all.

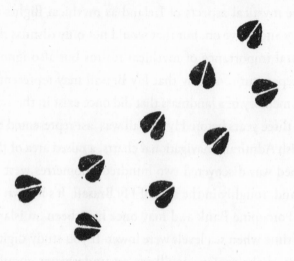

ROUTEWAYS

Lest we stray too far altogether into the realm of the fanciful, I'm going to direct us towards a more tangible remnant in the landscape, namely roads, which were the skeletal system on which society was built over thousands of years in this country. The mythologist Martin Shaw has written that 'underneath a motorway there was once a road, underneath the road there was a lane, underneath the lane there was a track and underneath the track there was once an animal path. Hoof prints under the concrete.'

It can help to bear this thought in mind as we roam through Ireland today. The routes that were used for

traversing the landscape are still evident if you keep a
keen eye out and open your mind to the rhymes and
rhythms of the land. Occasionally, as Shaw points out,
the tarmac you're driving on is built right over an ancient
slí, or trackway, and there are accounts from a century
ago of road builders removing broad flagstones that
would have had Iron Age chariots trundling across them,
and laying a new layer of gravel and macadam in their
place. Often, these new roads subsided once the solid-
stone flags from two thousand years ago were removed.

We're familiar with the idea of following the trail
of the great Roman roads through Italy, or the routes
through the Andes along which Inca messengers used to
run for days, bringing despatches throughout the empire.
I've trekked for miles along remote stretches of the Silk
Road in the far western provinces of China, sensing the
soldiers and scholars, traders and nomads who passed
along the route before me, yet we forget that there are
routeways remaining in Ireland from as far back as the
Bronze Age, three thousand years ago.

To encounter them you need to heighten your sense
of the lay of the land and realise that they tended to be
unsurfaced rights of way on which people made tempo-
rary pathways, building them up further when the
ground was wet or after floods and storms. The marshiest
sections were regularly re-covered with brushwood and
wattle mats, while shallow streams were forded with large

stones that needed resetting each year. Inevitably, some routes were better maintained than others.

Spotting these trails now requires altering your outlook a bit, as they don't always follow the expected route. Level terrain wasn't as important as land that was dry and firm, so that the light timber battle chariots that are such a feature of Iron Age tales wouldn't get bogged down or, even more so, the heavy cargo wagons, whose solid-oak wheels still occasionally turn up in bogs today. Another factor was the perceived safety of the route and whether it could be easily overlooked, as legal and military protection didn't extend far beyond one's own *tuath* (townland), and bandits roamed the wild lands in between.

When you scan the modern landscape, think back to scenes from old cowboy movies in which the hero passes through a gap in the hills or beneath a high bluff. Remember that pang of tension you felt as the soundtrack signalled a baddie waiting to pounce. Veering around or over these blind spots was often safer, even if it added hours to the journey.

Place names are a great tool for deciphering old routes through an area. The word *áth* means a ford over a river and marks a point through which the trail must have passed in an era before bridges. The names Adare, Athlone and Drogheda don't reveal much in English, but their Irish names offer us Áth Dara ('ford of oak'), Átha

Luain ('ford of Luan') and Droichead Átha ('bridge of the ford'). Each provides a definite geometrical point that can help track a road through landscape. Likewise, *droichead* in Drogheda means 'bridge', another feature indicating the intersection of a road with a river. You find it in Cill Droichid (Celbridge, 'the church of the bridge') and An Droichidín (Drohideen, 'the little bridge').

Ceis is a wattled path, *fearsaid* a sandbank and *tóchar* a flagged or timber causeway – all signs of a routeway long ago. The most common road word of all is *bóthar*, which meant a track that cattle can be herded along, or one that is wide enough for two cows, one standing longitudinally and the other with its bum to the first cow's flank. Ireland has at least 18 Ballinvohers, derived from Baile an Bhóthair ('town of the road'), and 24 Boherboys (from Bóthar Buí, 'yellow road'). There are also many Shanvohers (from Sean-Bhóthair, 'old road'), as well as Batterstown and Booterstown, which are both variations of 'settlement of the road'.

Another word that indicates a road is *bearna*, a gap or a pass the road would have passed through, as in Barnaboy, Barnbawn, Barnmeen and Lisdoonvarna. *Mám* means the same thing, as in the names Maumakeogh (Mám an Cheo, 'misty pass') Maumagarrane (Mám an Gharráin, 'pass of the grove'), Maumaratta (Mám an Rata, 'hollow of the young hares'), not to mention the seven places simply called Maum. They were all passes between the hills that a track would have naturally routed through. *Bealach* is another word for a way or a pass, but it isn't as high as a *bearna* or a *mám*. You find it in the names Ervallagh (Oirbhealach), Moyvally (Maigh Bhealaigh) and Baltinglass (Bealach Conglais).

By plotting all these words on a map, archaeologists have been able to discover the routes of our oldest roads, since most Irish place names are ancient and the information contained within them stretches back centuries. According to Dónall Mac Giolla Easpaig, the former Chief Placenames Officer, 'a significant number of place names date to before the seventh century'.

Hermann Geissel, a writer on historical geography who researched the old roads of Ireland, spent many years tracking the route of the Slí Mór ('great highway') from Dublin across the breadth of Ireland towards Galway by seeking out stretches of high ground and any traces of old road that might have linked them.[†] He pointed out that when an old road was no longer used, its area was subsumed into the land of the adjacent farms, and rather than both landowners moving their walls, they'd often agree to split the extra area between them, with one farmer moving their wall to incorporate half the length of the road, and their neighbour doing the same for the other half. Thus, sudden angular jumps in the line of a wall can reveal the presence of a now-vanished road.

† Hermann Geissel, *A Road on the Long Ridge: In Search of the Ancient Highway on the Esker Riada* (Newbridge: CRS Publications, 2006).

The routes revealed by these topographical points and observational tricks can then be cross-referenced with the great journeys recounted in myths to flesh out the direction of the trail. Storytellers made a point of anchoring their outlandish adventures in actual geographical locations and would, for example, provide details of the route along which a fleeing goddess fled in a particular direction from a known geographical feature, such as a route heading west of Brú na Bóinne, or east of the Knockmealdown, or between the Boyne and the sea.

This sleuthing has left us with evidence of several large trunk roads spanning the island during the Iron Age, and possibly before. Accounts from the old sagas, such as Bruiden Da Derga, tend to agree with this, even if they disagree with how many there were and the exact routes they followed. The old manuscripts claim that all roads centred on the royal ceremonial site of Tara, while some archaeologists believe it's more likely that they ran through Dublin.

Certainly, there's a thrill in standing at the very heart of Dublin, at the site of the original Áth Cliath (the ford of hazel or willow wattles over the River Liffey) and looking back along a road stretching southwards through the suburb of Donnybrook and across the coastal plains of Booterstown and Blackrock towards Bray in Co. Wicklow, and realising that this is one of the five great routeways, dating back over a thousand years. This is Slí Cualann, the route by which traders, adventurers and wandering poets passed through Dublin before the Vikings had even founded a city here in the ninth century.

The road continues northwards, out past Drumcondra and on towards Tara. Somewhere along that route it meets Slí Ascili, the trunk road that ran westwards to Lough Owel in Co. Westmeath, dividing the kingdom of Meath into a northern and southern part. There was a road heading north too, possibly as far as the Co. Antrim coast, called Slí Midluachra, and another heading south, like Slí Cualann but further inland. It was called Slí Dála and appears to have gone the whole way to Kilkenny. Finally, there was the most evocative and long-lasting route of all, the Slí Mór, which ran from Tara south-west to Clonard and on to Galway.

If these routes sound familiar to those who know Ireland, it is because they are remarkably similar to our modern motorways. Slí Cualann corresponds to the N11/M11; Slí Ascili and Slí Mór are precursors of the N4 and N6; Slí Midluachra is the N1/M1; and Slí Dála is the M9. While there were thousands of minor roads, there were only a few worthy of the name *slí*, which is a major highway on which two *carpait* ('chariots') could pass without one having to give way to the other.

The next-smallest road after the *slí* was the *ród*, on which at least one *carpat* and two riders could pass side by side. Then comes the *lámraite*, a minor road connecting two major roads; and a *tógraite*, which leads to a forest or river and can have tolls for people driving cattle on them. Finally, the lowest form of road is what we're left with today, the *bóthar*, 'cow road'.

It seems that just as the paved roads that stretched throughout the Roman Empire crumbled during the Dark Ages, so too did the major *slite* (plural of *slí*) degenerate, when the island was no longer as peaceful, wealthy or stable as it had been. The Iron Age stories from Ulster, such as Táin Bó Cuailnge, are laced with references to chariots and the major trunk roads needed for them, as are the accounts of the adventures of St Patrick and St Brigid in the fifth and sixth centuries; but then, by the time of the most common folk stories about Fionn mac Cumhaill and his Fianna warrior band, there were virtually no chariots at all. Fionn and his followers lived like hunter-gatherers, trekking through the forest and taking boats along rivers. It seems the glory days of Ireland's roads had passed.

It may appear odd that a country could lose its roads, but I witnessed this at first hand while travelling through the Democratic Republic of the Congo (then Zaire) in the 1990s. I realised that the roads I had read about in colonial accounts of the country from fifty years before were gone, having crumbled back to nature. It was Belgian oppression that had maintained the roads between Kinshasa and Kisangani, and in the years after independence they gradually eroded and were washed away; so too were the railway tracks lifted up and sold, and the runways allowed to crumble.

Likewise, the major routes through Ireland required strong central kingdoms to raise taxes and oversee their maintenance. That said, getting around Ireland a thousand years ago mustn't have been too challenging: the Vikings (who tended to use the rivers) and later the Normans never complained about bad roads. It was mainly the English in the sixteenth century who complained about them. They were supported by visitors from other countries in the eighteenth century who wrote reams about the lamentable state of Irish roads.

What is most remarkable today about these roads is that so much of them still remain as remnants in the landscape or references in old texts. There are over 1,660 surviving sections of *tóchair* (wooden causeways), some dating from 4000 BC and others maintained for over eight hundred years. Most of these are now buried, or slowly decomposing in land that has been drained or exposed, but all are mapped by the National Monuments Service and documented online at www.archaeology.ie.

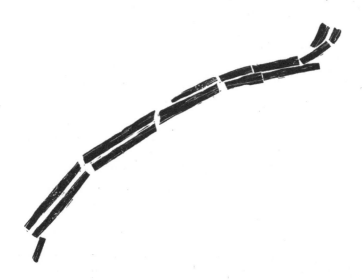

REALLY OLD ROADS

To get a sense of just how important roads were in early Irish society, open any of the mythological or historical accounts in ancient texts that are now accessible online.[†] So many of them, from Táin Bó Cuailnge to Accallam na Senórach to The Tripartite Life of St Patrick and to Mesca Ulaidh, refer to journeys, and this is despite the fact that only kings, poets, judges and semi-divine beings were allowed to travel beyond their home territory. In fact, a time-and-motion study of the old tales and the ancient Brehon laws of Ireland would reveal a kinetic whirr of almost perpetual movement. It's as if ancient Ireland were an ant colony, forever on the move.

† See the Corpus of Electronic Texts (CELT) at UCC, https://celt.ucc. ie/publishd.html.

You see it in the sagas of pre-Christian mythical warriors and in the love quests of fairy folk, as well as in the lives of the saints and the battles between the gods. Whether it's a malevolent scoundrel fleeing from the south of Munster northwards to Ulster or an aged warrior chasing his beloved around the coast – or an enraged poet, vengeful father or impassioned saint – it seems that everyone who mattered was on some frantic mission from one place to another. (Either that or stories about journeys are the most alluring and therefore the most enduring.)

There are six references to roads in Fled Bricrenn, the eighth-century tale about the hostel-keeper and troublemaker Bricriu, who invites three of the greatest superheroes of the age – Cú Chulainn, Conall Cernach and Lóegaire Búadach – for a meal and sets them competing against each other in the equivalent of a Marvel Comics mash-up that ended in the Oweynagat cave at Rathcroghan. Caithréim Conghail Cláiringhnigh, a tract about the fighting career of Flat-Nailed Conghal, has ten road references, and there are seven in the tale of Talland Étair, which recounts the journey of a psychopathic poet, Aithime, around Ireland as he abuses his poetic privilege to get people to do appalling things for fear he will satirise them and thus deprive them of their honour.

It's not entirely relevant to the topic at hand, but in southern Connacht, Aithime got King Echu to pluck out an eye from his head; and in Munster he insisted on a night in bed with Tigemach Tetbuillech's wife as she is giving birth. Then, in Leinster, he got to sleep with the high king's wife, the only condition imposed by the king being that no single Ulsterman could lie with her without his permission. Aithime duly had his way with her and then conspired to enable a rake of Ulstermen to molest her afterwards.

But it doesn't end there: before leaving the province of Leinster, Aithime planned to kidnap 150 queens, and he threatened the armies of Ulster to defend him from their furious husbands or risk humiliation by his pen. They dutifully obliged and a vicious, bloody battle ensued. When the Ulstermen were defeated and retreated to Howth, Co. Dublin, they were left destitute, with nothing to eat but clay, and brine to drink. Aithime, who had plenty of milk from his herd of seven hundred cows, dumped it over the cliff rather than share it with them.

All this shows the propensity for exaggeration in myth (or the sheer malignancy of poets) and this should be borne in mind when we read in old texts or law tracts that roads were always well maintained and cared for by local kings who ensured that their subjects saw to their upkeep and that a traveller, if injured because of poor road conditions, could claim compensation from him. There is undoubtedly some truth in these claims, but as with the accounts of Aithime's iniquity, we can't be sure how much.

For what it's worth, though, according to the laws, a king was required to make renovations to the roads in winter, before the great fairs and in times of war. An added incentive was that good roads increased the value of the surrounding territory. A highway leading to a monastery or the house of a lord added the value of three cows to the land along its margins. If the route led to a wood or mountain, the land was worth an extra cow, and if the land abutted a cow track leading to a cattle pond or another piece of land or a highway, it was valued at its base price plus the value of a two-year heifer.

There was no standard definition of what a road was to look like. It could be a series of trails running in the same direction through the landscape, like hiking routes today, or a fully realised linear causeway of dressed stone. Some were elevated on eskers (gravel mounds formed by the remains of ancient riverbeds that flowed beneath glaciers), while others were on the flat, with drainage ditches on both sides. A road of flagstones from AD 500–700 has been found in Bloomhill, Co. Offaly, and, as mentioned, more than 1,600 *tóchair* have been recorded running through bogs or swampy areas, the earliest dating from 4000 BC. Some of these bog tracks were maintained continuously over eight hundred years.

The road I'm most familiar with is three thousand years old. It's a *tóchar* that ran across Mayne Bog in Co. Westmeath and consisted of a wide trail of thick oak planks. It's not far from my home, just beyond the village of Coole. When I was feeling melancholic, I used to walk along it. And, to be clear, I'm not saying that I walked above it, or beside it, or where it had once been: I actually walked on the 3,000-year-old planks themselves. They were fragile and crumbling, but in some sections of the route they still looked like planks. Each had a square hole on both ends, which possibly were used to pin the plank with dowels into the bed of brushwood and branches beneath or to hold marking posts to delineate the edges of the track from the surrounding mire, like snow poles on modern road margins.

I was able to stand on it and even pick up bits and bring them home because, tragically, they were being milled into potting compost for use as soil in hanging baskets. Every time I went back, more had been churned up and destroyed. In a desperate bid to make some effort at preserving it, I used to gather up lengths of the oaks, but within weeks of their being removed from the moist environment of the bog, they crumbled to dust. I also tried writing about it in the *Irish Times*, but that proved to be another empty gesture. Neither the Government nor the public seemed to care that our heritage was being milled into peat moss.

When the *tóchar* was discovered in 2005, the National Monuments Service swiftly despatched an analysis team, which established that it dated from 1200–820 BC and measured up to six metres wide in parts. A small cohort of my neighbours were excited about the find, displaying that illogical pride we feel when some valuable piece of heritage has been found in our locality, even if we have nothing directly to do with it. We were all certain that the peat-processing company, Westland Horticulture, would stop extracting turf from the site immediately.

Alas, that didn't happen, nor did the National Monuments Service issue a preservation order. They didn't even record it in the Register of Historic Monuments. A spokesperson for the Minister for Rural and Community Development said, 'Given the co-operation so far secured from the landowner, it is not considered that further steps under the National Monuments Acts ... would be useful or warranted at this stage.'

And so that was that. Every summer, when it was dry enough for the massive peat harvesters to track out on the bog, the company would continue mulching this Bronze Age road into compost for use in flower baskets and window boxes. By 2018 at least three-quarters of the ancient road had been destroyed. It was only then that the Government forced the company to stop work and protect whatever remained of the road beneath the bog.

A similar discovery of a plank-built trackway elsewhere in Europe, such as at Wittemoor in Lower Saxony or at Flag Fen near Peterborough, is invariably deemed of great significance and often prompts the creation of

a local archaeology park and museum. Only in traumatised countries would the state decide that maximising
profits and maintaining industrial growth should take
precedence. This is because the connection with heritage
and with the legacy of those who preceded us isn't necessarily present in colonised societies.

This is particularly true in Ireland, where looking
back can spark a sense of survivors' guilt. Somehow,
we made it through the Famine and the centuries of
terror and oppression that preceded it. We modern Irish
people are the survivors of massacres by zealous Christian
missionaries against our native animistic beliefs and also
survivors of the raids by berserker Vikings high on alcohol
and hallucinogens, who for two centuries launched attack
raids to steal our wealth and womenfolk. And, of course,
there was the constant internecine warmongering of our
own tribes.

We'd like to think that the ancestors of our own
families always acted honourably and appropriately, but
the likelihood is that they didn't. Better not to think
about it at all and instead focus on copper-fastening our
own position in the world and amassing resources so
that we can be saved from ever having to endure such
troubles again.

There was a whole array of different types of road in
Ireland, from timber-planked linear causeways to stone
flags to basic earthen trails along well-drained sections.

The Life of St Brigid, written by Cogitosus in the seventh century, describes how they would 'lay a foundation of tree branches and rocks and some very solid earthworks in the deep and virtually impassable bog and in the sodden and marshy places through which a river ran.'

But what is most interesting is the uses the roads were put to. Cogitosus states that a road should 'bear the weight of the charioteers and horse men and chariots and wagon-wheels, and the rushing of people, and the clash of enemies on all sides.' Their primary use therefore seems to have been for transporting cargo and for allowing the movement of large numbers of people to fairs and gatherings – and, of course, for warfare, cattle rustling and tribal feuding.

ASSEMBLY SITES

The fact that our roads were primarily used for feuding and gathering for fairs and assemblies reflects the Irish character fairly accurately even today. We're no longer as bellicose as we once were, but the heaviest periods of road use are still during mass gatherings such as all-Ireland sports finals, music concerts and the national ploughing festival.

It's worth taking a look at the major Irish gathering sites, and the best way to do this is to turn to an active volcanic area, fifty kilometres east of Reykjavík. Humour me as we shift focus to an immense fissured rift valley where the striated cliff edges of the North American and

Eurasian tectonic plates can be seen facing off against each other – the very seam from which the two continents are pulling away from one another, a further two centimetres each year. At the base of the valley is a large open expanse surrounded by high mountains on three sides, with spectacular waterfalls and grass-covered lava fields running towards the gin-clear expanse of Iceland's largest lake.

This is Þingvellir, the gathering place of Iceland's ruling chiefs from about 930 to 1798. Each year thousands of people would gather here for a fortnight during the nightless days of June to set laws and settle disputes. It was the earliest version of a representative parliament – a full eight hundred years before the idea took root in Europe or North America. And still today, as you stand at the Lögberg (Law Rock) at the foot of the Almannagjá cliffs, where the law speaker recited from memory the existing laws to the assembled parliament, you can clearly hear how his words would have been amplified by the cliffs and naturally broadcast to the ruling members of each tribe.

The annual Alþingi ('parliament') held here was the social and political event of the year. The leaders and their entourage would trek for up to seventeen days over rough mountain passes to get here for a fortnight of debating, trading and score-settling, with plenty of festivities and socialising mixed in. There would have been hundreds, possibly thousands, of farmers, traders, artisans and entertainers here – all descendants of Norse and Gaelic adventurers, dressed in their most colourful clothes of the finest fabrics and with silk embellishments, according to the sagas.

None of this might seem relevant to Ireland today, but the fact that it continued up until relatively recently (I've known people who knew people who were alive in 1798, when the last gathering was held), before being abolished by the Danish crown, makes it easier to picture the great gatherings that also happened across Ireland, until so much of traditional society was wiped out in the seventeenth century.

Standing at Þingvellir today and looking out from the Lögberg at the stone foundations of the turf and wooden booths and encampments that were erected each year, and looking out at the lava fields that were used for grazing the animals that fed them over the fortnight, helps to summon up the great gatherings that were once part of Irish life too. The fact that the Icelandic landscape has changed so little over the centuries makes it all the more imaginable.

In Ireland you need to strain a little harder to summon up the great gatherings that were such an integral part of society. Until they were quashed by English oppression. The importance of such assemblies and the central role they played in satisfying the need to come together for revelry, bartering and trade is seen in the range of words to describe them. *Tionól* (an assembly, meeting or gathering) is the same as *aonach*, though the latter can also mean a fair or a hostile gathering. In contrast, *siamsa* means a friendly gathering, and *scoraíocht* refers to a festive gathering or an assembly. *Tuirling* can also refer to an assembly, based on its primary meaning, to 'descend' or 'alight'. It captures the idea of people gathering in from *na ceithre hairde* ('all sides') to a central place. *Feis* is possibly closest to an Icelandic Alþingi, being specifically a parliamentary gathering but also a feast or a convention. There is even a word for the practice of regularly attending fairs: *aonaíocht*.

No matter where you are in Ireland, you won't be far from the site of the local gathering place, and with careful observation you should be able to discern it in the landscape – whether it's *páirc an mhargaidh* (the market-place), *láthair thionóil* (a gathering place where assemblies were held) or *bánóg* (an area of level ground, often at a crossroads, that appears somewhat flattened by years of dancing). Nowadays, such sites are often used by the circus when it comes to town or for the annual community sports day or regatta, that is, if it hasn't already been sacrificed to commerce and sold off to a developer.

Occasionally, the site will be on low-lying land that is sodden and useless in winter but dry enough to be used as a communal space for the rest of the year, when most gatherings were held. Watch out for a piece of level land that doesn't seem to be owned by anyone – or, at least, is owned by everyone. These sites are often overgrown now and overlooked, but older members of the community can often still point you to the local places of trade and play and social cohesion.

These sites were then linked to larger regional and national assembly places, which are often recorded in folklore, with countless references to them in folk songs, old tales, bardic poems and ancient myths. If you look carefully you'll see them in the landscape – and, dare I say it, you can almost feel them too.

Possibly the most palpable and visceral site of all still today is the Hill of Uisneach, which was the great assembly point at the very navel of Ireland. It appears to have been linked to all the others by solar alignments on significant days of the year. But we should also explore some slightly less auspicious sites that are still visible in the landscape. They tend to be on hills offering extensive views over the surrounding countryside but are not so high that they are inaccessible. Words for 'height', 'hill' and 'mound' (*ard, cruach, mullach, cnoc, tulach*) are often incorporated in their names, and you'll find references to some of them in old manuscripts as being the inauguration site of ruling tribes.

Prof. Elizabeth FitzPatrick of the School of Geography and Archaeology at NUI Galway has identified many such sites, including Tulach Mac Amhalghaidh ('Humphreys' Hill'), the gathering place of the Magawleys of Calary, near Moate, Co. Westmeath; Ard na dTaoiseach ('Height of the Chieftains'), the inauguration site of the O'Dohertys on the Inishowen Peninsula, Co. Donegal; and Cruachain Ó Cupráin, near Killeshandra, in Co. Cavan, where leaders of the O'Rourkes of West Bréifne were proclaimed.

There's a site in Co. Meath that is principally known for its sports gatherings in the twentieth century but that had much more going on in previous centuries and even previous millennia. It's called Tailtin (Teltown) and is a large expanse of level fields leading to the River Blackwater between the towns of Kells and Navan. According to local lore and early monastic written accounts, this was one of the sites in which Lughnasa was celebrated over two weeks beginning in early August, with an extensive programme of horseracing, chariot competitions, boxing, wrestling and other athletic feats.

These competitions, known as Óenach Tailten, began as a way of honouring the life of one of the great goddesses who first moulded the land, Tailtiu. She was the daughter of the king of Spain and wife of the high king of the Fir Bolg, one of the Otherworldly tribes that were said to occupy Ireland before humans ever got here. When the semi-divine beings known as Tuatha Dé Danann invaded Ireland, Tailtiu married their leader and thus became foster mother to the god Lugh Lámhfhada ('Lugh of the Long Hand'), who was thought to be buried on the Hill of Uisneach and who was possibly a folk memory of a comet tearing through the sky. It was Lugh who first created the sports field for the games that were to honour Tailtiu's funeral.

According to the Lebor Gabála Érenn ('The Book of Invasions of Ireland'), Tailtiu died of exhaustion clearing the plains to make the land available for farming. That she came from Spain and helped to introduce farming seems to suggest that she is a symbolic representation of one of the waves of Neolithic or Bronze Age people who brought new skills and culture to the island thousands of years ago.

Before her death she asked Lugh to clear the woodland around the river so that there would be space for her funeral games. He began felling the old-growth temporal rainforest that once clad the land, and when she died he organised the event that became known as Lugh Nosad, the funeral games of Lugh. Written accounts record that they were held from at least the sixth century and appear to have continued on and off until the twelfth century.

Visiting the site today, you don't get the same visceral experience as at Þingvellir. Instead of an open expanse of rocky moonscape there's an array of pasture fields with native hedgerows and the odd bungalow and farmhouse; among all this is a scattering of grass-clad earthworks

and forts that now reveal little of their former importance. There are two parallel earthen banks built on top
of glacial mounds known as the Knockans. There are also
the remains of Rath Dhú ('Black Fort') and Rath Airthir,
which has three deep ditches and ramparts surrounding
it, revealing that it was an important site in the early
Middle Ages or the Iron Age. As is often the case in
significant gathering places, other important locations
can be seen from the highest point on the Knockans:
Loughcrew, Tara and the Wicklow Mountains are all
visible from the summit.

There's a tale of St Patrick turning up at the annual
games to ban them, or at least to break their connection
with pagan gods and bring them into the Christian faith.
In this account, Patrick was confronted by a pagan chief-
tain, Coirpre, who tried to kill him and had his servants
flogged into the River Blackwater. Patrick, in a fit of fury,
cursed the river and turned its waters black, which is how
it got its name, according to lore.

It was dusk on a cold autumn evening when I first
found myself in the area. I set about looking for remnants
of the church that I felt sure St Patrick's people would
have imposed on the region after his failed attempt to
Christianise it. I was returning from an afternoon gathering medicinal mushrooms, and the back seat of the
car was covered in fly agarics – the red toadstool with
yellowish-white spots known for its powerful healing

abilities and hallucinatory qualities, once the poison has been removed. I found myself lost down a tangle of lanes leading towards the Blackwater and had to ask a few local people for directions to the church. Each one pointed me in a different direction, and at first I felt they had seen the mushrooms and wanted to send me astray; but after heading off down numerous dead ends, a man in a jeep with doors tied shut with string told me that there were the remains of four Christian churches in the area. He said some of them had remnants of circular enclosures still visible nearby, suggesting that they date from the early Christian period.

Four churches in such a small area seemed like a concerted effort by St Patrick's followers to bring to heel those who had dared challenge him and to impose their control on the fun and frolicking of the games. They may have succeeded in doing so, but the landscape still flaunted its pagan past: in the graveyard of one of the churches, I came upon a rock outcrop with prehistoric art carved into it in the form of symbolic cup and ring marks, showing that the site had long been of ritual importance.

There wasn't all that much to see in the area, and had I not read the archaeological reports and numerous references to the games in mythology, I would have said that there were no remnants of a gathering place there at all. But the man in the jeep pointed out a few significant ridges and mounds in the fields. He assured me that local people were still keenly aware of the legacy of the place and mentioned a custom known as the Teltown Marriages, which his grandfather used to talk about. Unmarried people would come to the area at a particular time of year and the women would put their hands through a hole in a wooden gate in such a way that the men could see no part of them beyond their wrist. If a man had a good feeling about a woman or found her palm and fingers particularly attractive, he would clasp it in his own, and that was a sign that they would be wedded for a year and a day, after which time they were free to decide whether they wanted the 'marriage' to continue.

I asked whether his grandfather had witnessed this or had merely heard about it from others, but the man wasn't sure. I did find a more detailed account of the custom from 1836, written by John O'Donovan, overseer of the Ordnance Survey team who were then mapping the county. I wonder what the four churches would have made of the practice. They couldn't possibly have approved, and yet it continued right up to the nineteenth century. It was a good reminder that the grip that Christianity has had on the country was really only a post-Famine phenomenon.

HILL OF WARD

On my way home from Teltown that evening I got
caught in a traffic tailback in the one-street town
of Athboy just a few kilometres south-west of the games
site. I noticed a turn-off named Fair Green Road on
the map on my phone and wondered whether it could
once have been another one of the major gathering sites.
Then I saw that the road continued past the fair green
site to the summit of a low hill on a perfect east–west
orientation. At the summit it met the old road between
the towns of Kells and Trim, which was oriented directly
north–south. The orientation of an old road like that
was too accurate to be coincidence and I realised that

these roads probably met at some important point where people gathered coming from different directions.

The connection between the principal assembly sites and roads is seen most clearly in how the importance of Tara as a site of power and ceremonial ritual is often emphasised by the claim that five trunk roads met there, even if archaeologists believe that this may not be true. The law tracts also connect roads with assemblies, in laws such as the one that compels kings to maintain the roads in their kingdom for the great fairs. The biography of St Colmán Ela of Clonmacnoise cites a ten-kilometre tailback of chariots and other vehicles arriving to an *aonach* ('fair') at Clonmacnoise in the eleventh century, and that tailback didn't include those travelling on foot or horseback.

So, to avoid the traffic and to satisfy my own curiosity, I took the left-hand turn and, sure enough, just north of the old Yellow River (now the Athboy River) I spotted the abandoned fair green site: an uncultivated patch of ground, lush from centuries of animal manure and the debris of organic food waste. It's hard to gauge how old such a site might be, but the Irish name for Athboy, Baile Átha Buí, means 'townland of the yellow ford', and it's likely that travellers heading north-east from the ceremonial site of Loughcrew towards the monuments of the Boyne Valley would have used this spot to cross the Yellow River. It then became the crossing point for a few routes from different directions linking the settlements at Kells, Trim, Navan, Delvin, Oldcastle and Mullingar. And so it was natural to have a meeting place and fair green here.

The remains of cut-stone buildings reveal that Athboy was an important Anglo-Norman defensive bulwark from the twelfth century onwards, protecting the lands of Leinster from attacks from the north and west. Traces of the old fortified walls still exist, as does a grain mill that was later converted into a mill for timber. Historians estimate that some form of small settlement would have existed here since at least the sixth century.

Beyond the fair green the land rises to form a hillock that in other, less flat parts of Ireland would be categorised as a mere mound. The map showed that the road I was on continued right up to the summit, and I realised that this must be the Hill of Ward, a renowned assembly site of the Samhain festival. I had never set eyes on it, despite having lived only twenty minutes away for the past quarter of a century; but I had often heard stories and read accounts of it. At 118 metres tall it hardly impinges on the landscape, and none of the roads I had driven on in the area had brought me within sight of it. This is what I mean by referring to the fractal nature of the landscape and how it can concertina itself out to encompass much more than at first appears.

In its time, the Hill of Ward was a gathering site of far more significance than any fair green. In the year 1167 the last high king of Ireland, Ruaidrí Ua Conchobair, held a reform synod there that was attended by thirteen thousand horsemen and all the provincial kings, as well as important ecclesiastical figures, such as St Laurence O'Toole, Archbishop of Dublin; Gelasius of Armagh; and Cadhla of Tuam. While sites for markets and games had to be on level ground, the locations of the great gatherings for inaugurations and debates were often on sloped sites to allow for large crowds to amass and take part in a central spectacle.

I drove on up the hill, and after parking at the axial point where the north–south road met the east–west, I settled myself on a dry tuft of grass to gaze out over the undulating grassland of the Co. Meath plains. It was too dark by then to make out much of the surrounding countryside but I guessed that, despite the modest elevation, many of the most important ceremonial sites of Neolithic Leinster would be visible.

I headed home that night to sort through my mushrooms and set them drying on racks, but early next morning I was back in Athboy, taking the road up the hill again to see what more I could learn. Sure enough, from the summit I could see the Hill of Tara. It was 19km to the south-east, and I could also make out the ceremonial cairns at Loughcrew, 20km due north-west. Directly north, the Mahercam peaks on the Co. Cavan border, between Bailieborough and Kingscourt, could be seen, and beyond them was Slieve Gullion in south Co. Armagh, with the significant cairn known as Calliagh Berra's House on its summit. Beyond that again, in the north-east, were the Mourne Mountains. On the southern horizon I could see the Wicklow Mountains.

So, although the hill is barely visible in the landscape, everything can be seen from it. It would have made for a perfect assembly point for people from throughout Leinster and south Ulster, and indeed archaeologists have found that the grass bank I was sitting on is part of four massive rings of ditches and earthen banks that encircled the summit two thousand years ago. It seems that these were the outer barriers for some form of ritual that attracted great gatherings during the Iron Age. Finding ceremonial or defensive remains on hilltops is not unusual in Ireland, but there are few other sites with four concentric banks and ditches on a mound, apart from the Rath of the Synods on the Hill of Tara; Cruachán Brí Éile in Co. Offaly; and Ratra, near Rathcroghan, Co. Roscommon, which are all high-status sites.

This makes it likely that the Hill of Ward was once a place of great importance. Furthermore, there is written evidence by Geoffrey Keating, from the seventeenth century, that this was the location referred to in the mythology as Tlachtga, the site of a great *aonach* to mark the end of the harvest at Samhain and the beginning of the long, hard winter. Keating records that at Samhain, in the pre-Christian era, all the fires throughout Ireland were quenched and the druids would congregate here at Tlachtga to light a huge ceremonial fire. Embers were then taken from it to light a great fire at Tara, and from there all the fires of Ireland could be rekindled. Sitting on one of the four embankments that would have marked the outer ring of the ritual area, I could easily imagine the bonfires blazing on the hills of Cos. Cavan, Westmeath, Armagh, Down, Wicklow and Meath.

Evidence from a geophysical survey revealed a very large pit near the centre of the site, and this was confirmed by archaeological excavations, which showed proof of large fires having been lit here. They could have been the relics of arson during enemy raids or, later, of iron smelting, but it is also possible that they are remnants of ancient Samhain fires, as the site of Tlachtga is strongly associated with Samhain in the mythology. It is situated directly between two other major Samhain sites: the cairns at Loughcrew, which have a decorated standing stone that was positioned in the Stone Age so that the rising sun illuminates it at Samhain, and the Mound of the Hostages on the Hill of Tara, which was also laid out in the Stone Age to be in alignment with the Samhain sun. All three are Neolithic sites, and some have later Bronze Age and Iron Age construction on top.

SAMHAIN

People often wonder whether these ceremonial hill sites have any relevance to us today other than as archaeological sites. The farmers who own the land mostly find it a burden not to be able to reshape it to suit their agricultural machinery, and local communities have largely abandoned them unless there's an easy trail to bring their dogs or children for walks on. But the Hill of Ward, in particular, shows us precisely how such sites in the landscape can open us to so much more than themselves because of its strong connection with Samhain, one of the four quarter-day festivals that divided the year for herders and farmers for thousands of years. These quarter days are something we need to reconnect with if we are to begin the process of re-establishing our relationship with the land in a more harmonious and sustainable way.

Samhain marked the start of winter, when the harvest was saved and stored, and the cattle had been brought back from their summer pastures – a time when foliage dies back and harsh frosts and withering winds kill off plants and animals. It's also the basis of the modern festival of Halloween. Samhain was thought to be the time of the year when the threshold between worlds was thinnest. There's evidence that our ancestors regarded Samhain as the end of one year and the beginning of another, the equivalent of our New Year's Eve. In the same way, they believed that night preceded day, not the other way around, as we now have it. The long hours of darkness give birth to the dawn each morning, like a baby from the womb.

Samhain meant the beginning of a period of great darkness, with nature withering on the stalk and with the sun weakening and spending ever more time below the horizon – in the underworld. Darkness grew more powerful as it was fuelled and strengthened by entrapping the sun in its underworld realm for ever-longer periods of each day. It grew emboldened, such that creatures from the underworld, and the Otherworld, were able to access our world more easily. They lurked in the shadows and ventured to approach more closely, especially at night.

Their goal was to sneak through the temporal paradigm, from one realm to another, and the transition point between the years was an ideal opportunity.

The weakness in the space-time continuum in this period is why games of prophecy are still such a part of Halloween today. Finding the ring in the barmbrack foretold that the person would marry, finding a dried bean prophesied a single life, and finding a stick meant ending up in an unhappy marriage. These were messages from the future. Likewise, the single paring from an apple dropped to the floor revealed in its shape the initials of the person you would fall in love with.

There were many ways to take advantage of this weakening of the strictures of time and space at Samhain. Girls would enter a cabbage patch and pull a cabbage each. A cabbage with a bent stalk signified marriage to a hunched man; if the stalk was straight he would be tall and well poised. Another practice involved placing two hazelnuts on the fire grate and waiting for them to char and sizzle. If one hopped off like popcorn it predicted a broken relationship, and if both burnt away together it foretold a long-lasting match. There was yet another game in which hot lead or wax was poured through a rusty key held over a pan of water, the shape it congealed into forming the initial letter of the name of a future husband or wife.

These are just the recent practices that can be traced back a few hundred years, but they are likely to be far older and may even relate to events that occurred at Samhain thousands of years ago, as they do seem to resonate with them thematically. And we know from the old mythical tales that the weakening of the temporal dimension was matched in the spatial field, weakening the boundary between this world and the Otherworld. It was believed that fairies and other non-human entities could cross the threshold more easily. This may seem fanciful now, until we remember that the fairies are likely to have been remnants of the pagan gods and nature spirits – although some sources claim that the fairies are lingering energetic resonances of our more recent ancestors.

It should be remembered that the Irish word for fairies is *sióga* or *lucht sí* ('people of the burial mound'), from Old Irish *síde* or Middle Irish *sidhe*. It derives from the same Indo-European root words as the Sanskrit *siddhayoginī*. (*Yoginī* means a female master of yoga and Tantra, or a female deity in the service of the goddess Durgā. *Siddha* refers to an enlightened individual who has attained a higher spiritual state of consciousness.) Being able to access these magical forces was a potent thing. It's why my grandmother used to leave a *pláta caillí* ('witch's plate') of food on the windowsill for the Otherworldly beings, in case they got hungry while crossing realms.

Portions of the harvest crops would also have been left growing in the ground for them in what was known as the hare's corner, which was a patch of the tillage field that was left uncut to feed the earth deities. Alongside these fairies were ghosts, ghouls, pookas and shape-shifters. It's why we still disguise ourselves as the dead or evil spirits and head out into the night, roaming the roads, so that if we encounter a being from the 'dark side' they'll think we're one of them and pass right by. It was thought wise to appease these spirits with food too, which is why you can still turn up as a ghost on any doorstep in Ireland at Halloween and be offered sweets and nuts. We exported the practice to North America and it spread from there.

Going from door to door is the modern equivalent of my grandmother's *pláta cailli*, though hers was specifically for the *cailleach*, the witch – the most powerful force of all, the matriarchal spirit, the dark aspect (or shadow side) of the bright Mother Earth goddess. It was thought that she was the most likely entity to take advantage of the temporal and spatial anomaly of the inter-year night to sneak across the barrier into our world. This explains why the witch is such a central character at Halloween today. However, the *cailleach* is much more than a cone-hatted old woman on a broom. Originally, she was a divine being who was believed to have moulded the landscape and unleashed the rivers. It is she who instigates the darkness and destruction of winter.

These ancient ideas of Samhain that have somehow remained alive are referred to in our mythological tales as being associated with sites like Tlachtga, though it's hard to know what practices might have taken place at them. The solar alignments that occur between carefully positioned stone pillars at Neolithic sites on Samhain show us that the festival was important to our forebears five thousand years ago, and it appears to have maintained its importance through the millennia. Many of the central events in our mythology occur at Samhain, such as the initial invasion of Ulster in Táin Bó Cuailnge; the selection of Fionn mac Cumhaill as leader of the Fianna after he saved Tara from burning; the transformation of Óengus and his beloved swan-woman, Caer, into human form in Aislinge Óengusa; and the announcement by Óengus of his claim to the kingship of Brú na Bóinne in the tale of Tochmarc Étaíne.

It is often at the Samhain feast that warriors are offered poisoned drinks or challenged to a test of fealty or courage. The men of Ulster were said to hold a week-long festival of meetings, games and feasting to mark the day, and it was claimed that the mythical early invaders of Ireland, known as the followers of Nemed, had to give two-thirds of their children, their grain and their milk to the Fomorians, the malevolent supernatural race who were their oppressors at this time.

This latter story is the most outlandish, but it may also be closest to the truth, as it was common until recently for societies that lived in seasonal climates to kill off the fattened animals and those that might not make it through the winter, rather than bear the cost of feeding them through the winter. Offering some of these culled animals as sacrifices to the gods made practical, as well as symbolic, sense. The tale of Nemed's people and their sacrifices to the Fomorians is from the pseudo-history Lebor Gabála, compiled in the eleventh century. According to the mythology, the Fomorians were a monstrous group of marauding giants who may well represent the destructive aspects of nature: manifestations of storms, drought, deathly cold and darkness. Making offerings to them at the great fires of Samhain would therefore have been a form of psychological and spiritual defence against the destructive capabilities of a harsh winter, with its lack of light and growth. The excess animals and harvested crops sacrificed to them helped ensure that the benevolent gods would return with light, warmth and the vital forces for growth the following year. Animal sacrifice and the roasting of whole carcasses for the feast might explain the large quantities of animal bones found on the Hill of Ward.

The land helps restore our roots to these practices that were so important to our people and that may still have a role in guiding us towards a more sustainable relationship with the land. Neurobiological research is revealing the influence of seasonal variations in light and temperature on our neurological and psychological wellbeing. Mindfulness practitioners and scientific research appear to agree on the importance to our health of acknowledging the seasons and marking the transitions between them. Samhain, in particular, with its emphasis on the journey into darkness and the creativity and new life that can emerge from these fallow periods, is especially resonant.

Of course, some of the aspects of the old festivals can seem outlandish to us now, such as sacrificing animals; but people may think the same in the future about our dressing up as ghouls and witches at Halloween. And in fact there are accounts of bulls being killed and roasted for Samhain in parts of Co. Galway at least into the 1940s, and there's also the tradition of killing a cockerel or goose on the eve of St Martin's Day, 11 November. The feast day of St Martin of Tours was a popular Christian holy day throughout Europe that was possibly brought to Ireland by the Normans, but we seem to have used it as a cover to continue their practice of ritual slaughter and blood sacrifice.

According to numerous accounts in the Irish Folklore Collection, the sacrificial bird's throat was cut on St Martin's Eve and allowed to bleed into a bowl that was then used to consecrate a building as protection against the travails of winter and other dark forces. It's likely that the bird would have been carried around to the four corners of the building with the blood spurting from it. Accounts of this practice are recorded in the Schools' Collection – a massive gathering of folklore from the late 1930s – and the folklorist Billy Mag Fhloinn has collected many others.[†]

†   Billy Mag Fhloinn, *Blood Rite: The Feast of St Martin in Ireland* (Helsinki: Academia Scientiarum Fennica, 2016).

TLACHTGA

If I had heard that such an important heritage site of ceremonial ritual as Tlachtga existed so close to someone as the Hill of Ward does to me, without their knowing anything about it, I'd question their level of curiosity or connection with their surroundings. I don't really know how to explain my ignorance, except that in Ireland we have been cut off from the places that were once sacred to us, to such an extent that even those living nearby are often unaware of them. Certainly, the people of Athboy gave Tlachtga little attention until a group of spiritually inclined women began to re-establish the practice of ritual fires on the summit at Samhain in recent years. Their reigniting of the fire is part of a worldwide resurgence of interest in ancient sacred practices that has taken root in the last decade or two. It's an important development, even if there's often a lot of inaccurate history or pseudo-ritualistic practices connected with them, together with a tendency for bravado displays of egotism and elitism by some of the principal 'shamans' and mythicists who lead the charge.

In defence of my own ignorance, all I can offer is perhaps that Tlachtga was more clandestine than other sites. There was probably more effort made to hide the memory of it because it was considered a ceremonial site for specific spiritual rituals, as opposed to the Hill of Tara, which was an administrative seat of the *ard-rí* ('high king'), who regularly gathered his nobles and provincial chiefs there. Tlachtga was a place more for seers than for kings, so the Church would have made extra efforts to denigrate it and wipe it from people's memory.

Its spiritual importance is possibly why the Samhain fire was lit here first before being transported to the more secular site of Tara. The flame could have been carried in a bundle of smouldering mosses or fungi along the Athboy River to where it meets the River Boyne near Trim and from there downriver to within a few kilometres of Tara.

As I sat on the hill one morning, I consulted my phone's satnav and noticed something else interesting, which I've since seen corroborated by archaeo-astronomers. There's a direct line between the rising sun at Samhain and the quartz standing stone in Cairn L of Loughcrew, and it passes westwards straight through the earthworks at Tlachtga. If traced eastwards the same line also pierces Lambay Island, an important Neolithic site for the production of stone axe heads and a point in the Irish Sea from which the rising sun would have emerged dramatically (and symbolically) from the pitch-darkness of night.

Therefore, the path of the sun's rays links together these potent places of spiritual intensity. But here it's even more evocative, as the name Tlachtga appears to mean 'earth spear'. *Ga* is still the word for spear today, and *tlacht* has been translated as 'earth', although it also means 'covering', 'protection' or 'hide'. The first part of the name could also come from *lacht* ('milk yielding') or *leacht* ('grave mound' or 'memorial cairn').

But the consensus seems to be that it translates as 'earth spear' and refers to lightning, which is fitting because Tlachtga was originally a fiery goddess whose death on the hill led to its name. She has a rich and convoluted backstory about inflicting damage on people with her long, destructive pillar, which was named Cnamhcaill ('bone damage') and could blind those who gazed on it, deafen those who heard it and kill those who touched it. Much like lightning. She was even accused of having slain a Christian martyr, but these stories may well be the fantasies of medieval monks who wished to besmirch this powerful goddess and let their imaginations run riot in the cloistered darkness of the scriptorium.

Perhaps permission was given to them to be especially lurid when transcribing the oral literature concerning her. She was a particular threat to the Church because she represented a hill that was still a nexus of druidic practice. At least, this is what was claimed about the hill in a book by Geoffrey Keating from the seventeenth century. He wrote that 'the druids of the four provinces of Ireland gathered there to offer sacrifices to all the gods'. This idea was supported a century later by John Toland, who wrote: 'All November fires in Ireland were called Tine tlacht'd-gha, after that place in Co. Meath where the arch-druid of the realm had his fire on said eve.'

And so the monks wrote sensational stories about how Tlachtga and her father, Mog Ruith, learnt malevolent skills in Jerusalem from the first Christian heretic, Simon Magus, and even invented a flying machine called 'roth ramach' that was shaped like a wheel and powered by lightning. Mog Ruith was even alleged to have beheaded John the Baptist. This appears to have been a classic case of character assassination, and the only detail that might be 'true' about Tlachtga's dramatic backstory is that her father was Mog Ruith, since that fact is mentioned in a few texts, such as the Dinnseanchas and the late-medieval collection of women's lore Banshenchas.

Mog Ruith means 'devotee of the wheel', and since scholars believe the wheel is a reference to the sun, his name is just another way of describing him as a seer. There are other accounts of his being recognised as arch-druid of Munster, who, after outclassing all the druids assembled by King Cormac mac Airt in the third century, gained the rank of arch-druid of all Ireland.

It's hard to tell if any of this had any bearing in fact, but there was just one point that the Church was keen to communicate about Tlachtga: she received her come-uppance in the end, experiencing a violent and humili-ating downfall. It's the same message we've encountered so often already on our journey, that powerful women who dare to assert their sovereignty end up impoverished, molested, shamed or dead.

While accounts differ about Tlachtga and her father's outlandish exploits, they all agree about the multiple sexual assaults she experienced that led to her death three seasons later. Three men attacked and raped her at the festival of Bealtaine, and nine months later, at Samhain, she gave birth to three boys on the high land above the ford at the Yellow River before dying in childbirth. This sounds like a tragedy, and on one level it is, but the minute you read of three men, nine months and three boys, you realise that this story is likely to be a code for something else. There is some sacred insight being communicated through the numbers that would have been discernible to those in the know.

For us now, it just raises our antennae and makes us look more carefully at the surviving evidence. The information contained in her story was seared into the landscape at this site, which was named in her honour, and it kept its name of Tlachtga until the middle of the seventeenth century, when the landowner, a Mr Ward, was evicted during the campaign of Oliver Cromwell, and his name became associated with the hill.

According to the mythology, Tlachtga's sons grew up to be rulers of Munster, Leinster and Connacht and were named Doirb, Cumma and Muach. It was said that as long as their names were on people's tongues, Ireland would be safe from foreign occupation. Regrettably, the names were forgotten and now exist only in dusty tomes. As a result, the country succumbed to its fate.

Now that we are in the process of remembering these names and reconnecting with the sites in which their energy is still latent, there's an opportunity for great renewal. For the message of Tlachtga's life and death appears to be the potential for rebirth after death. Of all the goddesses, she is the one most strongly associated with Samhain, which is a celebration of death that leads three months later to the resurgence of new life. Her death on the hill led to the birth of three new beings.

She is the daughter of the druid most associated with the sun and so, in turn, is a representative of the sun herself. The sun dies every night and is reborn at dawn. She is a potent figure strongly connected with the number three and its multiple nine, which signifies completion and harmony in some traditions.

Our ancestors consciously built into the year these times when we can reconnect with something bigger and grander than our own minor dramas – periods and events in which we can take time off to reset ourselves and replenish our stores, hearts and minds. And redirect ourselves, once again, towards our true course in life. Many of these stories are trying to remind us that we are manifestations of consciousness, inhabiting a physical body, and that at times we can reach through the veil and contact a wider realm, a deeper awareness.

Samhain is all about taking a pause when the work has been done and the winter food and fuel are safely stored. It's a time to pan out from the narrow concerns of humdrum existence and remember that time and space are an illusion – that more expansive realms lie beyond. With our winter needs for warmth and nourishment seen to, we can allow ourselves the luxury of turning inwards to the timeless, internal realm, where we can be far more than the sum of our daily activities.

These insights are particularly apt at this moment in history, when we seem to be at a Samhain-like intermediary period of our existence. As the natural order of things is thrown into disarray in what appears to be a 'between time', between the old world and the new, there is solace to be got from sites like the Hill of Ward, which remind us that there are times when there is the potential to access insight and energies that we wouldn't normally have.

Nowadays, whenever I hike up to this hill above Athboy, I like to picture every light and flame in the countryside being extinguished on the eve of Samhain, and the darkness spreading throughout the world. For this one short period, the shadow side, the underworld, the unknown realm was given its dominion and allowed to seep through into our reality, to imbue everything with the cleansing, obliterating abyss of darkness – for just a little while.

And those living in that beyond, dark realm – our beloved dead ancestors – were also then allowed to seep back temporarily into our world. It was a time of uncertainty and some fear, until with great ceremony and celebration, possibly even within the walled ditches where I like to lie on the hill, the fire was relit and was given to flame-bearers to spread across the island.

The flames became a signal that we had successfully returned from our period of interaction with the underworld and the denizens of the Otherworld, and we were stronger and better for it. The spirits of our ancestors could now be welcomed back into our homes with safety. They posed no threat to us. We had shown our respect to them and they would now be helping us as we entered the chasm of darkness and death of deep winter. For the next few months the sun would lurk beneath the horizon for most of the day (in the underworld), and the *cailleach* of winter would unleash her storms and fury on the land. We'd make it through, because we had the dead now on our side protecting us. All would be well, and soon spring would come again. Spring will spring.

MYTHS

The crucial lesson from all the convoluted stories we've explored so far is that, while our current understanding of landscape is of something external – something that is 'out there' – this was not always the case. The internal idea of territory is just as important, if not more so. This is a common concept among societies that have not been torn from their traditional beliefs.

The anthropologist Keith Basso has quoted an Apache elder in Arizona saying that while 'white men need paper maps', the Apache 'have maps in our minds'. We in Ireland also had maps in our minds. They were passed down through the mythology, which is why place names are a crucial component of old tales. Our history is rooted to place in such a way that the location of an event is almost as important as the event itself.

The great linguist and anthropologist Harry Hoijer described something similar in Navajo culture, in which 'even the most minute occurrences are described by Navajos in close conjunction with their physical settings, suggesting that unless narrated events are spatially anchored their significance is somehow reduced and cannot be properly assessed.'

History has not always been about the deeds of bellicose men and the chronologies of battles: at one time it chronicled the yearly processes of tribes interacting with their surroundings. People who are truly connected with the land will focus as much on where events occurred as on the details of the events themselves. We know that the iconic freedom fighter Michael Collins was killed in Béal na Blá in Co. Cork, but few of us can agree on what happened.

This is why place names are so important in Irish mythology. Our ancestors made these names, and they had purpose behind them. By saying them today we are 'repeating the speech of our ancestors', as Charles Henry, a Western Apache expert says.[†] We are summoning up locations that they too knew. And the names cannot lie. They show what is different and what has stayed the same.

† Keith H. Basso, *Wisdom Sits in Places: Landscape and Language among the Western Apache* (Albuquerque, N. Mex.: University of New Mexico Press, 1996).

Like old photographs, they record the land as it was in a previous era. It's something we can cling on to when the narrative in the myths becomes altogether too bewildering.

It is worth bearing with the myths, though, even when they are at their most far-fetched. There is almost infinite information being imparted in these tales; deciphering it requires us to look at the land and all of reality through a fresh prism. Irish mythology is based on the notion that the natural, human and divine worlds all co-exist, overlapping one another and with different elements becoming subordinate at different times. That's a lot to get one's head around. That each story can be read in different ways, with different conclusions, depending on how you choose to interpret it, is bewildering to our increasingly linear minds.

The scholar Marion Deane has done great work in deciphering their seeming irrationality and indecipherability. She has mapped out the parallel worlds that are often being addressed and the points at which they coalesce in myths such as Compert Conculainn ('The Conception of Cú Chulainn'). A few different accounts of this tale have been preserved by monks who wrote down oral versions in manuscripts over a millennium ago.

In a version from the first half of the eighth century that was recorded in the lost Book of Druim Snechta, we learn of King Conchobar mac Nessa and his Ulstermen hunting a flock of birds across the plains in the era before ditches, walls and dykes were imposed on the land. 'Nine score birds' had devoured much of the grass and herbs in the kingdom down to the bare roots, and so nine chariots were sent after them. They chased them south from Emain Macha across Sliab Fuait, to Edmand and Brega.

The birds were shackled to each other by silver chains but were able to keep moving south until night fell and winter swept in. Because the snow was heavy the Ulstermen had to pause for the night, unyoking their chariots and spreading out to seek shelter in this strange territory. Eventually they found a bare and uncovered house that had an unsettling appearance. In a back storeroom was a woman in the pangs of childbirth. Conchobar's chariot driver, Deichtire, who was also his sister, went to help her. She acted as midwife and nursed the baby when it was born.

In the morning the house and birds had vanished and only the baby, a little boy, and their horses remained. So they took the child with them, and Deichtire cared for him as her own son until he fell ill and died. Deichtire was devastated, but while she was mourning his death she happened to swallow a small insect from a vessel she was drinking from and became pregnant. Lug mac Ethnend (a form of the god Lugh) came to her in a dream to say that he was the tiny creature in the water. He had also been the boy that she had reared, and it had been he who guided them to the strange house. He told her that

he would be born from her womb as a baby boy named
Sétanta, who in time would become the divine warrior
Cú Chulainn.

Now, I realise that's a lot of story points to take
in – there are more shifts and turns and illogical leaps
than we are comfortable with in modern tales. But bear
in mind that the story would have been told with elaborate description and numerous digressions over a series
of nights, or even weeks, and people would have heard it
each year of their lives and would have focused on whatever was most relevant to them for that time, like the
way we grow up with the often illogical and farfetched
antics in *The Sound of Music*.

The key points of this story are that the Ulstermen
hunt the wild birds until forced to shelter in a mysterious
place where a child is born who proves to be of mysterious provenance. All was well with this, except that the
Ulstermen were worried that people would think that
Deichtire's brother Conchobar was the father of the baby,
as her habit was to sleep next to him at night. So they
arranged that she would marry a farmer who was not of
the elite warrior class, and she managed to abort the baby
and become pregnant straight away again by the farmer,
giving birth to Sétanta.

That's the extent of the story. It's dreamlike and
poses as many questions as it answers, but primarily what
is missing for modern audiences is an understanding

of all the symbolic elements, such as the silver chains between the birds, the need to unyoke and dismantle the chariots, the pregnant woman in the back storeroom, the nine chariots chasing nine score birds and the fact that they travelled south over Sliab Fuait, near Newry, to the territory of Brega, where Cos. Louth, Meath and Dublin are now.

It's open to all of us to intuit the meaning behind these mysteries, though we need to bear in mind that the meaning won't necessarily be rational, as oftentimes the subconscious mind is being addressed as much as the conscious one. Marion Deane observes that the name Deichtire stems from *deg thír* ('good land') and so represents the goodness and bounty of the land. King Conchobar, as the great king of Ulster mythology, can be equated with the sun, and Lug, as a warrior god often associated with crafts, but also with light, can be seen as a brother or alter ego to him.

The fact that the story is set during the onset of winter – when the land has been laid bare by the absence of sun, and the birds have also stripped the land bare, and the house is bare too – seems to point to this being about the growing seasons of the year and how the darkness and cold of winter (when the great flocks of migrating geese appear from the north) force us to unyoke our plough and seek shelter, in the hope that new life may be born again and prosper when the sun returns.

The woman, in the form of the land, is shown to mate with the sun and have offspring through the intervention of the light, but that offspring weakens and dies. Only when the farmer is introduced and he cultivates and impregnates the land does it bear healthy, long-lasting fruit. He too is shown to require the help of Lugh's light or skill to do this.

The sun riding through the land in his chariot is reminiscent of the stables for the 'solar' horses found on the Hill of Uisneach (Lugh's resting place) in Co. Westmeath. It was said that Dagda, one of the gods of Tuatha Dé Danann, used to pull the sun across the sky in a chariot. It's also reminiscent of the prehistoric depictions of ceremonial 'solar chariots' that were believed to carry the sun across the sky each day.

It's hard to say that any of these interpretations are correct. Scholars are battling it out about what meanings can be taken from the tales, but in the meantime we are free to interpret them in whatever way is most meaningful to us. By their very nature, none of them can be conclusive. They are all just ideas and potentials that can be accepted or discarded at our own discretion. The land is communicating with each of us in different ways, and we are all interpreting that communication differently. Our relationship to our environment is a subjective and personal thing.

ENCOUNTERING
ÁINE

I want now to bring us on a deep dive into one particular part of the province of Munster to explore just how resonant and multifaceted any individual region can be. It's an unassuming and overlooked part of south Co. Limerick near the border with Co. Cork that has deep and discernible connections with prehistoric rituals and traditions of energetic transformation.

The central animating source at the heart of this area is a serene and picturesque lake called Lough Gur. It may not be as spectacular or elemental as the Atlantic seaboard or the mountains of Co. Donegal, but from a mythological and ceremonial standpoint its potency is hard to overestimate. Even those of you who know Ireland well may never have heard of it, and yet my hope is that it will permanently alter how you experience your surroundings.

The lake itself is in the form of a narrow horseshoe, about 1.5km long, with reedy banks and calm shallow waters running to boggy patches of scrubland and grazed meadows. It's enclosed by a protective circle of limestone hills that hide it from all those who don't specifically go in search of it. You'd never stumble accidentally upon Lough Gur.

In Irish its name is Loch Goir, *goir* being the genitive of *gor*, meaning 'incubation' or 'hatching'. What this area represents is a region through which new energies are birthed into the world. That's a rather grand statement, and *goir* could simply derive from *gearr* ('short'), but let me make a case for the more evocative derivation.

We first need to realise that the lake didn't always look as it does now. It had a neat round hill rising from its centre that looked conspicuously like the bump of a pregnant woman, until drainage works were carried out in the area in the 1840s, exposing some of the lake bed and leaving the hill surrounded on only three sides by water. This hill is called Knockadoon (Cnoc an Dúin, 'Hill of the Fort') and its smooth, stretched-belly sides are now less apparent, being clad in mature ash-dominated woodland on the eastern side, with oak and hazel mixed through it. In the now-dry lake bed vast numbers of ritual offerings were found embedded in the soil: shields, axes, tools and, most especially, ox bones that are thought to have been hurled into the water as ceremonial gifts to the goddess Áine, who was believed to manifest part of herself in the form of this lake.

The concept of such manifestation is hard for us to grasp today. I first encountered it when my car broke down one stormy Sunday morning as I was on my way from the Dingle Peninsula to fetch a nucleus of Irish black bees from a breeder in Tipperary. I rang roadside assistance, and the mechanic said he'd be an hour at least getting to me. He advised me to knock on the door of the nearest house to find shelter and stay warm. It was a friendly area, he said, and anyone there would invite me in.

In the way one does when suddenly cast adrift from one's carefully made plans, I took his advice and walked to a small nineteenth-century worker's cottage, where an elderly man beckoned me in out of the rain. I had only got as far as the hallway when he recognised me from a television documentary I had made about the Mosu matriarchal tribe of Yunnan Province in China fifteen years earlier and said with a hint of urgency in his voice, 'Look, there's something I need to show you down the back, here.' He led me straight through a dark and cramped kitchen space to a back room that was clammy with dampness and had mildew creeping up the walls.

I looked around, wondering why he had led me to this grim place that was entirely empty, apart from a large old tea chest against the gable wall. He apologised about the state of things, saying that no matter how hard he tried to heat the room, he failed, and that any attempt to install an electrical socket in it would short circuit the rest of the house.

I nodded and was about to return to the relative warmth of the kitchen, which had a Stanley range, when he blocked my path and began pulling the crate aside and then beckoned me to stand directly in the centre of a flagstone that it had been covering. I noticed that he was careful not to approach the spot himself as he directed me where to stand, with my back to him, facing the gable wall. I did as he asked and instantly felt the most unusual sensation running up my spine. It was like a chill that ran from my coccyx straight up into my skull and made me feel nauseated, but there was also a mildly expansive, buzzing type of sensation in my forehead that was more pleasant. I stepped back off the flagstone again and immediately the feeling vanished, and the nausea subsided.

'What the hell was that?' I asked.

Carefully repositioning the crate over the flagstone, he said, 'I thought you'd have come across something like it in all your travels.'

I assured him that I hadn't, and his shoulders dropped a little. We both fell quiet for a moment, and then he said that he felt it was somehow connected with the goddess Áine, who was linked to many old stories and place names in the area. He explained that he had inherited the cottage two decades before from a relation who had lived there alone and had always kept the back room empty except for the carefully positioned crate. He had never thought to ask her about it when she was alive, but since she often talked of Áine and used to recount songs and stories about her, he had a hunch it might be connected with her.

'No doubt you heard of the mother goddess in all your time in them places out foreign?' he said, and I nodded. 'Well,' he said, 'we had the self-same thing here. To the south we have the Paps of Anu, and further east back along the road you'll be travelling to get your bees you have Knockainy. That was her principal residence on this earth.'

It was the first time I had heard of Knockainy, but back in the car later I realised it was just six kilometres east of Lough Gur and was indeed on the road I'd be taking to get the bees. In Irish its name is Cnoc Áine, meaning 'Hill of Áine'. Áine was a protagonist in mythological tales throughout the province of Munster and, as we saw, may have been at the root of the name Shannon (Sean-Áine).

'As far as I can tell,' the man said, 'she was regarded as the power behind the sun in these parts long ago. And so, naturally, she was connected with the fertility of the soil too. If you spend any time around Knockainy, the people there will tell you how important she is to them.'

'Is she still worshipped there?' I asked.

'No, no. Nothing like that,' he answered gruffly, 'but they know about her. She's in the landscape. Her mind is in the hill there, and her womb, of course, is in the lake.'

'In Lough Gur?' I asked, and he nodded.

The idea had intrigued me, and I was keen to find out more and also to find out if he believed some other part of her was in his back room; but just then the mechanic rang, saying he was at the car and wanted me to unlock it. So I had to rush off and we never got to finish our conversation. I was late already for the beekeeper, and I didn't want to risk losing out on getting some native bees to enliven the mostly mongrel mix of bees I had back in Co. Westmeath.

I didn't have time that day to explore the area around Lough Gur and Knockainy, but as soon as I got home and had the bees settled in their new hive I started looking into the story. I came to realise that it was true that Áine was the closest thing we have in Irish culture to the idea of a mother goddess. The word *áine* means 'delight', 'pleasure', 'agility', 'melody'. It is the genitive form of *án*, meaning 'bright' or 'brilliant'. Some scholars including T.F. O'Rahilly, considered her to be the same as, or a sister goddess to, Gráinne, who was regarded as a deity of the *grian* ('sun'), which produces the *gráinne* (the harvest of grains of corn). Both can be considered aspects of a divine female figure who represents the animating life force of nature.

The point the man had made about her being represented in the landscape became clearer to me when I read about the mountains he'd mentioned near Killarney, the Paps of Anu. These were related to another aspect of Áine. Not only was she regarded as a manifestation of brightness and pleasure, but for the poets of Munster (and their druid forebears) she was considered a prime source of inspiration or nourishment. It is claimed that the poets would routinely shut themselves off from the world by blindfolding themselves or isolating themselves in a darkened room to seek inspiration in her esoteric realms. And it was not only poets but musicians, dancers and writers who sought creative expression through Áine in the part of Munster over which she most had sway, Sliabh Luachra ('Mountain of Rushes'), part of the old Kingdom of Luachra.

Sliabh Luachra sounds like a physical place, and it is, more or less; but you won't find it on any map. It is as much a state of mind as an actual location that stretches over a wet, marshy mountain area of rushes and bog willow along the Cork–Kerry border. It's within the energetic influence of the Paps of Anu, which are a pair of breast-shaped mountains topped by nipple-shaped cairns between Killarney and Ballyvourney. Their Irish name is Dá Chích Anann ('the two breasts of Anann'), with Anann referring to the goddess Áine.

These mountains are the most evident physical manifestation of Áine in the landscape, and their aura was believed to evoke a heightened energy of creativity and a blending of realities between this world and the next that poets, healers and those who dabble in Otherworldly forces have always sought to tap into. A central factor in the poetic ability of my great-great-great-great-granduncle Aodhagán Ó Rathaille, the renowned bardic poet of the seventeenth century, was that he was born and reared within the magical mists of Sliabh Luachra. And still today the style and excellence of music and dancing from this region are esteemed.

It may seem as if all this is tangential to Lough Gur, but what I'm hoping to make clear is how Áine was represented within the landscape at prominent geographical points in the centre of Munster. The Paps were Áine's breasts, Knockainy could be considered her heart or head, and Lough Gur was her womb. Whether there was some part of her in the man's back room, I'll never know. I've never been back since and I imagine he might no longer be alive, but the house probably still stands.

From what I've been able to gather from old legends in the area, it was from deep within the lake that Áine created new life, which was then nourished on her teat in the Pap mountains. This idea of seeing the landscape as a fertile, life-giving female is common in cultures in which indigenous wisdom still exists. In particular, the worship of topographical features that resemble the reproductive organs or elements of maternity in the landscape is a common trope of prehistoric cultures throughout the world.

It's clear that there's been a significant shift away from this way of seeing the earth towards our current exploitative, destructive methods that never seek to ask the earth's permission to engage with it, or to even attempt to work in harmony with it. It helps to bear all this in mind as we approach any once-sacred landscape such as Lough Gur.

LOUGH GUR
LEGENDS

Every seven years Lough Gur is said to disappear entirely and be replaced by a single supernatural tree that appears magically from the lake bed. That the lake transforms into a tree is particularly resonant because it chimes with another central story about Lough Gur and Knockainy that concerns two gods from the Hill of Uisneach at the centre of Ireland. These gods were Uainide and Eogabal, *uainide* meaning 'green' and *eo-gabal* being made up of *eo* ('tree') and *gabal* ('fork' or 'gable'). So, we can infer from this that woodland and the verdancy of nature are laying claim to ownership of the goddess of light and life, Áine, or that she is the progeny of their loins. Probably it is the latter.

It can take a moment to grasp concepts like these, as we're no longer accustomed to mythological thinking. But it does spark the question of who actually did give birth to Áine and to the lake. According to some legends, it was an old woman, presumably an older version of Áine herself, because gods are timeless and non-linear. They just exist.

This old woman was noticed by St Patrick having a pee on the roadside. Or as the *seanchaí* Ned Hynes told the Irish Folklore Commission in 1971,

> there was a poor oul' woman makin' her water, in pardon to you. And he [St Patrick] said 'God increase you!' And she kept on making it away until she made the Lake. And the Lake was coming all around her.

That this story is a lot older than 1971, or even than the time of St Patrick in the fifth century, is clear from its similarity to the far more ancient tale of the horse belonging to the god Aengus of Newgrange who is said to have urinated Lough Neagh into existence. But let's focus here on the magic tree that the lake is transformed into every seven years. As we've seen, a tree in the mythology of any culture is often far more than it seems. In Ireland it can represent the very core of existence and consciousness, an umbilical cord through which life energy can flow. The tree that Lough Gur was transformed into was said to have been covered with a *brat uaine* ('green cloak'), which is likely to be an echo of the original god Uainide, who claimed part ownership of, or kinship with, the hill of the lake goddess, Áine.

At one of these seven-yearly events when the lake had just disappeared and been replaced with the tree, an arrogant young man came riding by and tried to steal away the cloth that covered its branches. He grabbed hold of it and tried to flee, but an old woman was hiding there keeping watch beneath the cloak. She was sitting placidly by the trunk knitting, and when her presence was revealed she immediately began to call out:

> Chughat, chughat, a bhuaine bhalbh!
> Marcach ó thír na mBan marbh.
> A' fhuadach an bhruit uaine dhom bhathas.

> (Awake, awake, thou silent tide!
> From the Dead Woman's Land a horseman
> rides.
> From my head, the green cloak snatching.)[†]

† Recounted by an anonymous elderly woman from Askeaton, Co. Limerick, on 24 April 1879 and reported by David Fitzgerald in *Revue Celtique IV* (1879–80), pp. 186–7.

This old woman was likely to be a manifestation of Áine, or else her words of alarm alerted the goddess and immediately she brought the waters flooding back in, rising up so swiftly that even before the rider had managed to reach the edge of the lake bed the back half of his horse was washed away, and with it went the *brat uaine*, back into the depths of Áine's domain. It was said that if the man had succeeded in stealing the cloak, the area's enchantment would have been lost for ever.

This story seems to suggest nature rising up to protect itself from exploitation by humans, and this same message is echoed in another tale about the lake's guardian, who emerges from the depths of the lake to sit at her lakeside observation point while combing her golden tresses with a golden comb. She represents nature and the energy of the land. One day a young *buachaill* (which can mean 'boy' but in this case means 'cowherd') secretly watched her, entranced by her allure, and soon found himself coveting her comb. He kept spying on her from the hillside until she fell asleep, and then he crept down and stole it from her.

The image can be taken as a metaphor for how farming stole the earth's gift of a natural bounty of food for all beings and tried to commodify it and limit the bounty to farmers and their families at the expense of all other creatures. Farming is basically a system of scratching and clawing on the surface of the earth, to reshape it in servitude to us.

In the story of Lough Gur and the young *buachaill*, it is said that from that day on there followed years of hardship and tragedy in his life as the forces of nature took revenge on him until eventually, in old age, he gained some degree of self-awareness and realised he would have to make amends for taking something that didn't belong to him. He returned to the lake and dropped the comb back in. Suddenly, all was right once again. I like to imagine that this implies that we can heal our broken bond with nature by making the necessary amends and that things will restore themselves quickly into balance. But maybe the tale is just trying to get us to return things we steal.

There is, though, one message that emerges clearly from all the Lough Gur stories, and it's to do with the mother goddess's relationship with the rational, exploitative, colonial world. Ask anybody in south Co. Limerick or north-east Co. Cork about the folklore of Lough Gur, and they will tell you two things. Firstly, the lake is an entranceway to the Otherworld, and vast layers of non-human existence are accessible through it. Secondly, the most famous human to have been transported into this supernatural realm is Gearóid Iarla, the son of the first coloniser in the province, whose arrival in the fourteenth century led the way for all the other oppressors and exploiters who came in his wake.

Gearóid Iarla's father was Maurice Fitzgerald, first Earl of Desmond, and it is said that he came upon Áine by the River Camoge one day just east of her hill at Knockainy, beside a rather crude bridge that she is said to have built at Cloghaunainy (or Clochán Áine, 'Áine's Causeway' or 'Áiné's Stepping Stones'). Maurice sneaked up on her as she was combing her long hair on the riverbank after bathing. 'He advanced noiselessly on her from behind, knowing that if he had but possession of the cloak, he would have her in his power, and he seized it before she was aware of his approach.'[†]

Once he had taken her cloak she admitted that she was now powerless to resist him and that she couldn't stop him having 'his will with her'. The cloak could be a metaphor for her hymen, or for nature's willingness to temporarily submit to abuse by humans if we are short-sighted and craven enough to attempt to do so.

Áine tells the earl that she will bear him a son who may not be entirely of this world and who oughtn't to be questioned about anything strange or sinister that he may do. And so from this violent act comes the remarkable character of Gearóid Iarla, who is destined not to belong entirely in any world. There are almost as many tales about him as there are about Áine.

When dealing with a character like Gearóid Iarla, we need to contend with the fact that the dividing line between mythology and history in Ireland is blurred. While the Romans saw their mythology as historical, the

† The story was collected in the area by a descendant of Gearóid Iarla, David Fitzgerald, and published in *Revue Celtique IV* in 1879.

Irish people tended to think of their history mythologically. We never quite replaced one discipline with the
other and simply melded them together. Gearóid was an
actual Anglo-Norman lord, born Gerald FitzMaurice
FitzGerald in 1335 and confirmed by King Edward III
as third Earl of Desmond on the condition that he marry
Alianore Butler, granddaughter of King Henry III.

The history books relate that Gearóid Iarla (Iarla
meaning 'earl') took control of his family's vast estates in
Munster that had been forcibly taken from indigenous
families. He was appointed Lord Justice of Ireland in
1367, with responsibility for enforcing the infamous laws
of cultural genocide known as the Statutes of Kilkenny
on the people of Ireland. The statutes consisted of 35
prohibitions forbidding colonisers from trading with
the Irish people, having marital relations with them
(including lovers or adoptions), practising Irish games,
practising Brehon law, speaking Irish or interacting in
any way with Irish singers, poets or musicians.

There are many counter-tales, however, of his refusal
to adopt the ways and customs that were expected of
him. He was charitable to his subjects and supported
Irish culture by giving money to poets and bards. He
even composed poems of his own, initially in Norman
French but then increasingly in Irish. He was impris-
oned in 1370 for defending a local Irish lord, and while
there he wrote some accomplished poems, some of which

survive in the Book of the Dean of Lismore, compiled in
the first half of the sixteenth century. Among Gearóid
Iarla's poems is the proto-feminist 'Mairg Adeir Olc Ris
na Mnáibh' ('Speak Not Ill of Womankind'). In it he
defends women and urges men not to dismiss or deride
them, pointing out that, unlike men, they are not a
destructive, exploitative force on earth.

> Ní dhéanaid fionghal ná feall,
> ná ní ar a mbeith grainc ná gráin;
> ní sháraighid cill ná clog;
> mairg adeir olc ris na mnáibh.

> (Bloody treason, murderous act
> Not by women were designed.
> Bells o'erthrown nor churches sacked
> Speak not ill of womankind.)

Somehow, he managed to walk a tightrope between
the Anglo-Norman and Gaelic worlds, which ensured
the loyalty of poets and keepers of lore over the six-and-
a-half centuries since he lived. More significantly, he
existed between the earthly realm of his father and the
Otherworldly existence of his mother. That he was a
demi-god, both human and supernatural, is what really
led to his continuing renown, and it's demonstrated
in countless stories of his magical abilities, including

performing sorcery, shapeshifting into some disturbing forms and jumping into a bottle of wine as a party trick at a banquet, which led to his banishment from his father's court, who was embarrassed, appalled and frightened by his son's abilities.

THRESHOLD LAKE

When we hear accounts of Gearóid Iarla transforming himself into a bird and being pounced on by a cat, or flying through the sky with a coach and horses, or skating at night on wafer-thin ice, or hitting a sliotar so high during a game of hurling that he had time to offer all his teammates a pinch of snuff before the ball descended from the stars again, all that is truly being communicated is that magic exists in this world. None of it is really about Gearóid at all. He is a motif on which to hang a deeper truth.

The whole story of his divine lineage is, of course, make-believe. Maurice, first Earl of Desmond, never actually slept with a goddess, and Gearóid was in fact born to Maurice's third wife, Aveline FitzMaurice. The stories were propaganda, probably paid for and disseminated by the Desmond tribe to strengthen their hold on the area, as it was known that overlordship or kingship depended on the male claimant sleeping with the territorial goddess. The tale was an attempt to copper-fasten the legitimacy of their colonial occupation.

Distinguished Munster poets and storytellers profited handsomely from composing these stories, and they based the tale on a far older one that survives today in an eighth-century text about the king of Munster, Ailill Ólom. According to the tale, the king went for a snooze on Áine's hill at Knockainy during the festival of Samhain one year, and when he woke he realised that the entire hillside had been stripped of grass while he slept. This incident so intrigued him that he sought out the poet and prophet Fearcheas mac Comáin in Leinster for an explanation. Fearcheas couldn't cast any light on it, but they both returned to Knockainy for the following year's Samhain feast to see whether it would happen again. (As we've seen, it's no coincidence that this melding of the real world and the magical happened at Samhain, when the threshold between worlds was weak.)

Ailill dozed off again, but Fearcheas kept vigil, and after a time he saw Áine appear on the hillside along with the King of the Fairies. Immediately Fearcheas leapt up and murdered the fairy king, which startled Ailill awake. When his eyes fell on Áine he was overcome by her beauty, and his lust grew so strong that he decided to rape her on the spot.

Áine endured the ordeal, but afterwards, in fury and anguish, she tore off his ear. She purposely inflicted a non-fatal blow, as she understood that, once maimed, a king could no longer continue in power, since his subjects regarded his disfigurement as symbolic of the weakness of the natural world, of which the king was a personification. He was forced to give up his crown, and from that day forth he was known as Ólom, from *ó* meaning 'ear' and *lom* meaning 'stripped' or 'bare'. It is said that he died about AD 235 a broken, impoverished man.

The Earls of Desmond, as the new ruling Anglo-Norman dynasty occupying native lands, came to realise that in Munster it was the goddess of sovereignty, Áine, who bestowed sacred power on kings. To be accepted, they needed to prove direct lineage from her, and so they paid someone to tweak the old tale, making sure to manipulate it so that Áine would give consent to Maurice and therefore have no reason to disfigure him.

This is why we get so much of Gearóid in the tales surrounding Lough Gur. It's all just clever brand-building by the Desmonds more than six hundred years ago. It was a form of cultural colonisation, just as the monastic scribes had made sure to weave St Patrick into the old pagan folklore once Christianity began to spread in Ireland after the fifth century.

For us to understand the full energetic potency of the place, we need to filter out the figures of Gearóid and his father. There are deeper truths seeking to be expressed that lie just beyond these tales. We can get a hint of them in stories like that of the young woman Gearóid encounters on the lake shore one day and observes picking up a ring from a stone. As she does so, the waters rise up red, like blood. When she screams and puts the ring down again, the lake subsides.

Stories like these that are hard to make sense of usually have the most potency. This particular tale echoes other accounts of significant women in the area who let out a scream – there are tales of the flooding of the lake being caused by the screams of Aveline FitzMaurice, Gearóid's mother, and by his wife, Alianore Butler – which brings forth a flood of destruction from the lake. It may simply be a reassertion of the idea that the entire area is composed of Áine's body and that she can manipulate the physical reality as easily as we can blink or bleed from a pricked finger, but there is likely to be a lot more to it.

What we do know is that for our ancestors the lake represented far more than a body of still water. In the area that was drained in 1837, huge numbers of ox bones were found in the mud of the former lake bed, suggesting ritual slaughter over a long period. 'More than one hundred cartloads of bones were removed and sold to dealers,' wrote Prof. Robert Harkness in 1869, and during the Famine years he claimed that even more bones were dug up and sold to collectors by impoverished local people.

Not only were bones dropped into the lake as offerings but so too were Bronze Age chariot fittings, shields, bone pins, axes and finely smoothed stone discs. Prof. Michael O'Kelly of UCC noted in 1942 that 'there is scarcely a museum or private collection in Britain and Ireland which does not include some objects from the lake and its vicinity.'

That the lake was an orifice – an opening into another dimension – is clear from the countless stories dating back thousands of years and right up to the present day of energetic beings emerging from the lake and of humans entering other dimensions through it. Gods and goddesses would regularly appear on or above the lake, or nearby on the shore, as would a silent coach and horses, and an Otherworldly hunting party, and a black bull seventeen feet high with a backbone as thin as glass, and the entire fairy horde of Munster. Well-known figures were lured into the fairy realms beneath the lake for games of hurling or to play music, as happened to the famous piper Seán Ó hAodha, who spent a night playing for the undead in a palace below the water with 'shoals of freshwater fish gazing in admiration through the window of the enchanted banquet hall', according to a tale in the Schools' Collection.

It's clear that the Church was aware of the energies around Lough Gur and was discomfited by them. One tale collected in 1939 from Clonakilty as part of the Schools' Collection tells of how St Patrick was warned about a very large serpent in the area. While in Cashel he made a side trip to chase it off and banish it into Lough Gur, ordering it to remain there until the Easter Monday before Judgement Day.

This brave and decisive act by Patrick was supposed to signify the end of 'pagan' beliefs in this part of Co. Limerick, but the clergy evidently still had concerns. Although the serpent was now safely confined to the bottom of the lake, it was known that every seven years it would arise again to wonder how long more it had to wait until the last day on earth.

This seems to hint at the fact that a degree of nature worship remained alive, just beneath the surface, and the Church was aware of its threat. The prevalence of these pagan beliefs is not always immediately apparent, since the Christian monks who were responsible for documenting the vast majority of our folklore and history up until the twelfth century did their best to avoid mentioning them. Yet Ireland maintained a strong connection with the gods of the land, the water, the stars and the sky while also practising Christianity.

It may be a leap to suggest that the serpent in Lough Gur represented a feminine deity, but in many cultures a serpent is symbolic of the lithe, flowing energies that run through the earth and that are believed to be able to guide us towards higher consciousness. It represents the antithesis of the male-controlled viewpoint of the Church.

There are many such examples of stories that the Church would have seeded in the culture to emphasise that the female energy was now dead. The pub on the shores of the lake was run by a local councillor and was known as the Red Cellar until it was burnt down some decades ago. Its name is taken from a nearby cave where a massacre was committed during the Cromwellian era, but in fact it earned its name from a bloody murder that happened long before that, according to the local story-teller Ned Kearns, who recounted that an old woman used to go there to do her sewing while keeping watch over the lake. One day a local hunting band, the White Boys, saw her trail of red thread running across the land-scape. They followed her up to the cave and murdered her there. That's the extent of the story. It's not deft or gripping, but it makes its point once you realise that the woman is likely to be connected with the old woman who was knitting under the tree and the young woman who combed her tresses by the lakeside. All are versions of Áine.

The White Boys, too, need to be deciphered, as they are not the land-reform agitators of the eighteenth century but the mythical Fianna warriors, a 'pagan' hunter-gatherer band who finally came to heel and converted to Christianity at the end of their days, according to accounts that the Church attempted to spread. Michael Dames has suggested that the story could signify the murder of Áine as sun goddess, 'when the last red threads lining the clouds are extinguished in deepening twilight'.[†]

† Michael Dames, *Mythic Ireland* (London: Thames and Hudson, 1992; republished as *Ireland: A Sacred Journey* in 2000).

STONE CIRCLE

One must be careful not to get lost in the weeds of mythology when considering the Irish landscape. We need to focus on what remains on the land, as this is why Lough Gur still holds such allure today. The stories have their place, but archaeologists have found remnants of the lives that were lived here over eons. Bones of bears, deer and arctic lemmings were found in the Red Cellar floor dating from before humans ever settled in Ireland, and there are remains too of the Mesolithic hunter-gatherers who arrived here from Britain nine thousand years ago, possibly via the Shannon estuary and the Comogue River.

A walk across Knockadoon Hill will bring you to the foundations of houses built by the Neolithic people who replaced the hunter-gatherers six thousand years ago. The visitors' centre is a reconstruction of the mud-walled houses they built on stone foundations, with their deeply overhanging thatched roofs that are reminiscent of houses found everywhere from Africa to Afghanistan. Wooden posts were driven into the ground and these then supported a hipped roof and screens made from woven hazel rods known as wattle. The screens were covered in a mixture of dung, clay and straw that when dried was waterproof and may then have been insulated with a layer of straw, reeds or turf.

Soil samples and archaeological findings reveal that these first settlers, who were relatively small in stature and had a life expectancy of less than thirty years, would have cleared the land with stone axes to create pastures for cattle and fields for cereals, which grew well in the warmer, drier climate of the time. The grain would have been milled on a saddle quern to create rough meal for porridge and flatbread. They would have hunted geese, ducks, gulls and coots; gathered hazelnuts, crab apples and wild berries; and fished for eels, just like their fore-bears at Mount Sandel in Co. Derry. Archaeological remains also reveal that the area was a hive of activity of tool-making and fishing and that the dead were mostly buried in a nearby wedge tomb, although some children seem to have been buried within the house enclosures themselves.

Yet by far the most visceral and evocative physical artefact in the landscape is a ceremonial site that has somehow been preserved for over three thousand years just up from the lake. It is called Lios na Gráinsí, or Grange Stone Circle, and consists of 113 standing stones arranged in an almost geometrically perfect circle. Not only is it far larger than any other stone circle in Ireland, but the massive stones form a continuous ring, each abutting the next to create a space 45 metres wide backed by an earthen bank 9 metres wide and about 1.2 metres tall. It dates from about 5,500 years ago, but the embanked enclosure surrounding it is older again.

If you haven't been, I urge you to go there and just stand in the centre and feel what you feel. Beneath your feet is ordinary grass, but beneath that again is a smooth floor of yellow clay. It has symbolic markings set into it in gravel pebbles. It's not visible, but it's there. You somehow sense it, just as you also get a palpable feeling of otherness at this site. The whole circle is 'charged'.

But if 'feeling' isn't your thing, there's plenty to notice too, such as the fact that the stones are not all equal. Some are larger and taller than others. Of the 113 stones, a dozen stand out from the rest. These massive slab-like uprights are positioned directly opposite each other, forming axial points that appear to be in communication with each other, or at least in balance.

Opposite the main entrance passage, you might also see that two stones are set together to form a V-notch. On the cross-quarter day of Samhain, the setting sun passes through this notch, before running directly across the centre of the circle and down through the entrance passage and out onto Lough Gur, the opening into Áine's infinite realm.

It's hard to claim anything about solar alignments and astronomical interpretations with certainty because some of the smaller stones at Grange were set in place again in the nineteenth century, and the change in the angle of the earth's tilt relative to the sun over thousands of years needs to be factored in too. Gauging the sun's alignment with objects positioned in the landscape is a subjective matter, dependent on where you're standing, and archaeo-astronomers are now casting doubt on some of the alignments that were claimed for these sites in the past. Frank Prendergast, for example, has been conducting pioneering research and developing computer models to track the site in relation to celestial bodies.

Nevertheless, there does seem to be a clear alignment between the sun and a squat, triangular-topped stone next to the V-notch stones, as is demonstrated by a study done by the photographer Ken Williams, who specialises in documenting Neolithic sites. On cloudless evenings at the Samhain cross-quarter day of 8 November, Williams has taken dramatic photos of the sun streaming down the passage and casting a shadow of the pointed stone that lines up with the entrance and marks the exact spot where the sun sets. It's a spear of light cutting through the circle on the eve of Samhain and connecting it directly to the lake.

For some reason this site that is clearly and indelibly connected with the Mother Earth goddess or sun goddess Áine is also linked with Samhain, an annual festival marking the end of the harvest and the beginning of winter. The principal ceremonial construction has been designed to lure people here on one evening of the year in particular, the winter cross-quarter day, when the harvest has all been saved and the old year officially dies. Legend has it that the most elaborate Samhain festival in Munster was held here.

It is said that at one time there were four or more circles at this site. Some of them were possibly even more extensive than Grange Stone Circle, but we can really engage only with what we see, and there's plenty to hold our interest here, especially the biggest stone in the circle, an enormous boulder that stands just to the north of the entrance passage. This is Rannach Chroim Dhuibh, which translates as 'the division of Crom Dubh (Black Crom)'. It's a flat-faced, 55-tonne slab of rock that stands 2.5 metres tall, with a further 1.5 metres beneath the ground.

In one sense it's just a normal rock of volcanic breccia that forms part of the circle, but the fact that it was dragged to this spot from 1.5km away and appears to form an alignment with the sunrise at the summer solstice makes one take notice. And although it could be entirely my imagination, whenever I approach it, I experience a sense of disorientation or dizziness that is unmistakable. It seems to palpitate with a resonance that is both calming and energising. If you visit the site you'll probably find yourself drifting over to it intuitively. You'll end up gazing up in a sort of blissed out way. At least, that's how I notice people behaving there.

Beyond all the speculation, there are some things of which we can be reasonably certain. The site was created for some form of ritual or ceremony, most likely at Samhain and possibly also at midsummer, which is when most people still gather there today. The huge amount of broken pottery discovered here makes it clear that large groups of people used to assemble within the circle. Many of the sherds date back beyond the current layout of the site to the Early Neolithic period, which suggests that it has been a ritual site for millennia and for the people who lived here before our lineage even considered migrating across from the Pontic Steppe six thousand years ago.

The chief archaeologist for the site's excavation in the 1930s was taken aback by the extent of the heaps of broken beakers at the foot of some of the stones. He surmised that they were the result of a ritual involving the drinking of beer followed by the deliberate breaking of the vessels on the pillars. There was feasting too, as is clear from the deep layers of organic debris dumped immediately behind the triangular-topped stone and its V-notched neighbours.

So, this was a site of ritual. Great feasts were held here and they were connected with the sun and its relationship with the earth. But I believe we are still missing some crucial insights, and my feeling is that the cliff-face rock of Rannach Chroim Dhuibh can offer them.

CROM DUBH

A lthough Rannach Chroim Dhuibh is just a massive hunk of rock without any markings etched on it, and although it has only the roughest quadrangular shape to it, it still reveals a fair amount through its name, which we can presume to be ancient, as *rannach* is an old word meaning 'divisive', 'dividing' or 'staff'. We know that Crom Dubh is a personification of one of the principal gods, Crom Cruach. Until a generation ago he was still being honoured, to some degree, on the Sunday of the harvest festival at Lughnasa.

It is Crom Dubh who is thought to have first brought wheat to Ireland, which is why he is *crom* ('bent' or 'crooked'), from carrying the weight on his back, and *dubh* ('black' or 'dark'), from journeying beneath the earth into the winter underworld of Gráinne–Áine's subsoil to find the grain and bring life to it. His dark colouring could also have been a folk memory of our predecessors, the dark-skinned Neolithic people who originally brought grain to Ireland.

Certainly, being both dark and crooked made Crom Dubh a suitable contrast to Lugh, a god often associated with light and sun, and then later to St Patrick. Crom Dubh and his alter ego, Crom Cruach, represents the shadow side of pagan belief, as is demonstrated in a text of the Dinnseanchas that alleges that people offered up their firstborn child to him in return for a plentiful harvest in the coming year. The children were killed by having their heads smashed on a stone idol in Co. Cavan that was believed to represent Crom Cruach, and their blood was then sprinkled around its base. Visiting the stone circle today at Killycluggin, amid the lakes of Co. Cavan, where the cult stone was found buried in the ground, is a disconcerting experience, as the grass there seems unusually lush and fertile, as though still being fertilised by centuries of blood sacrifice.

Certainly, the Killycluggin stone must once have been associated with unpopular things, or was at least seen to be standing in the way of 'progress' or the advancement of other ideas or figures, because it has been deliberately smashed in two by a hammer or crowbar, after which it was scorched in a bonfire and buried. Local lore claims that it was St Patrick who smashed it. Archaeologists have been able to identify the spot on which it stood: a flat-bottomed pit that had been deliberately sunk into the subsoil to receive it. I'm not sure if they tried testing the soil around it for excessive residues of bacteria and pathogens from human blood, but I believe such things are possible.

Because Crom Dubh is principally associated with the grain harvest, it's no surprise that his stone would be positioned so that the rising sun appears right on top of it on the dawn of the summer solstice, a marking point in the growth of the grain crop. Nor is it any wonder that the next alignment of the sun with the stone would be on the day of the festival of Samhain, which marks the end of the harvest. In fact, the whole circle can be considered a solar observatory.

The only question is why the other two significant dates in the harvest are not also marked, namely the start of the sowing season at Bealtaine (1 May) and the beginning of the harvest at Lughnasa (1 August). But in fact the eminent researcher of stone circles Jack Roberts has made the case that particular axial stones in the circle are indeed aligned with these cross-quarter days of Bealtaine and Lughnasa, when they are observed looking out through the entrance from inside the circle.

The calculations needed to achieve this would be challenging for most of us today. Imagine what it took four thousand years ago!

Crom Dubh is therefore definitely synonymous with the grain harvest. In her comprehensive survey of Ireland's harvest folk belief, *The Festival of Lughnasa* (1962), Máire MacNeill found references linking him to harvest time throughout the country. He was one of the dominant gods of the land until St Patrick, and even into the middle of the nineteenth century the weekend after Lá Lughnasa (Lammas Day, 1 August) was known as 'Friday, Saturday and Sunday of Áine and Crom Dubh.'[†]

Why would Áine be linked with Crom Dubh for these Lughnasa harvest festival days? Because it was she who, as the earth goddess of land and sun, joined with Crom Dubh, purveyor of grain, to create the staple of life – bread – and to provide the crops that would keep animals alive through the dark winter when this stooped god and beautiful goddess descended back into the underworld.

Occasionally in the mythology a woman accompanies Crom Dubh as his mistress, plaything or ward, and her name is Eithne. It just so happens that *eithne* means a grain kernel or the fruit of a plant. So, the big rock you find yourself gravitating towards at Grange has something to do with the magical transformation

† *Transactions of the Kilkenny Archaeological Society*, Vol. 2, No. 1 (1852).

that happens when sun, earth and seed combine in a sacred alchemy that happens between the spring festival of Bealtaine and the end of the year at Samhain to produce enough food for when the sun goes to sleep in winter and the earth turns barren. These are potent forces that our people have respected, and even worshipped, for thousands of years, right up until recently. This is why a loaf of bread is such a symbolic item – whether at a Christian Mass, at Jewish Passover or in the temple rituals of Ancient Egypt.

THE BULL

Grange Stone Circle is the most dramatic physical remnant of all the epic and bewildering layers of heritage and history around Lough Gur, and the most significant mythical element connected with it is the bull, that most allegorical of beasts. We started our exploration of Lough Gur by considering the female energy there; it's fitting that we end it with the male.

In the panoply of Irish gods Crom Dubh can be considered the most testosteronal of all. In fact, in stories he is often contrasted with the bright, shining Lugh of the elegant and long, dexterous arms, or with Manannán, the luminous sea god with his bright white waves of curling locks and a dandyish propensity to fly across the sea in his winged chariot. The hunched, grimy, blood-drinking figure of Crom Dubh has more of the animalistic male characteristics to him. His primary fixation is hauling his seed around and spreading it as widely as possible. He'll sow it into any open furrow he can find. His fate is to follow in the hoof prints of the oxen and bulls who coax the shy earth open with their long, pendulous ploughshare so that his seed can then be slipped in to impregnate the earth.

In light of this, it is no surprise that many of the old stories depict him with a bull – a special bull that comes back to life no matter how much 'progressive' forces like the Church try to kill it. In the archives of the National Folklore Collection, and even in the living lore of places like Corca Dhuibhne (where I experienced Áine in the back room of the old man's house), you'll find countless stories of St Brendan or St Patrick or other 'enlightened' change-makers combating Crom Dubh and attempting to kill off his bull, the principal manifestation of his manhood. In these stories, no matter how much they try, the old bull comes back to life again. Even if only his broken bones and bloodied hide remain, he re-emerges.

This connection between Crom Dubh and his bull casts further light on the two cooking hearths and the few cattle bones unearthed in the enclosure, as well as on the mounds of food remains found behind the

Samhain-marking stones. And, of course, on the piles of oxen bones cast into the lake.

Throughout Europe and Asia, cattle were used as sacrificial animals, replacing the humans who would have been sacrificed earlier on in appreciation of a good harvest and hopes for similar benevolence in the future. November was the ideal time to offer up spare male cattle, when their use on the farm was complete and there were not enough resources to feed them through the long winter. Much better to use their meat in ritual feasts that would strengthen the community before the harsh times, and by offering libations of the blood and bones to the earth they could also propitiate the gods. As we learnt earlier, around coastal regions of Co. Galway there are relatively recent accounts of families skinning and roasting a bull in honour of Crom Dubh at Samhain, and animal sacrifice continued as part of St Martin's Day in November.

The bull and oxen are as central to Grange Stone Circle as Crom Dubh and Áine are. Indeed, there's an intriguing argument that the reason that this is the only stone circle in Ireland in which the megaliths form a contiguous circle, creating an unbroken barrier, is that it's actually a bull ring. At Samhain of each year, the argument goes, Crom Dubh, in the form of a bull, was led down the stone passage and into the ring for a series of ritual displays or games before being slaughtered and roasted at a feast involving copious drinking from clay mugs that were then smashed on the stones – as clay offerings back to the earth.

There is a tale from the nineteenth century about how Áine emerged from the Otherworld accompanied by a red bull at Samhain. Once again she found herself raped by the Earl of Desmond (or the bull, in some versions) and so gave birth to Gearóid Iarla nine months later at Lughnasa, just as Crom Dubh impregnates her at Bealtaine and she brings forth her offspring of grain at Lughnasa.

These tales are circuitous and tangential, but that's just the way of mythical realities. In the last few centuries we've been wooed into simplistic narratives, but don't think that those are in any way a more accurate interpretation of reality than these looping, far-fetched snippets of mythical anecdote. Both are just avatars for the inexplicable.

ANCIENT GAMES

Allow me to tie up some loose ends about Lough Gur before moving on. My own feeling is that the bull ring interpretation of the unbroken stone circle there is unlikely to be correct, although I wouldn't be surprised if one or more head of cattle, or icons representing cattle, were paraded through it. We know that the site was used as a solar calendar to help calculate the best times to till the land, sow seed and harvest the crop, and it's clear that it was also used for ceremonies or ritual feasting; but if it did have another use, it could well have been as a threshing ground.

Throughout the world, in such places as Ethiopia,

Crete and Mongolia, I've seen stone-lined circular spaces with a level floor on which sheaves of cereal were scattered. Animals, with cloth on their hooves, were then allowed to tramp on them to separate the grain from the husks and straw. In Greece people danced on the grain in these circles, which had high sides so the wind couldn't blow the grain away.

This might account for why a level floor of yellow clay was packed down to a depth of sixty centimetres on top of the bare ground at Lough Gur, and it also chimes with its current name, Grange (or Lios na Gráinsí), from the Indo-European *gre-no* meaning 'grain'. It might also explain why three symbolic shapes were outlined underneath the clay using carefully positioned limestone rocks. The shapes themselves are open to interpretation, but they may well represent a ploughed furrow, the *rannach* ('staff' or 'divider') of Crom Dubh, and a crescent moon, which would tie in with Áine's characterisation as the moon goddess, carer of crops. Both the moon and the *rannach* are of precisely the same length, 36.4m long, so they seem to be in resonance with each other.

If you asked people long ago how the Grange Stone Circle had been created, they would have readily replied that it had been carved out by Crom Dubh dragging his long, heavy *rannach* through the earth to open up this circular portal – this orifice in the mother earth. His staff is a phallic appendage, just as the other great god, Dagda, had his club, which was called *lorg* ('cudgel', 'stick' or 'staff').

This then gives rise to another intriguing notion that there was a tradition in the prehistoric age of playing a type of hurling game around Halloween, or Samhain, with long sticks that had a bend at the end of them.[†] In the old law tracts and sagas at least two types of stick-and-ball game are referred to, and both sound somewhat similar to hurling or hockey. The stick used in one game is called *camán* ('bent thing') and in the other is known as *lorg áne*, with *lorg* meaning 'stick' and *áne* meaning either 'driving animals or balls' or 'of Áine'. In fact, the modern word for hurling, *iománaíocht*, maintains this sense, with *iomáin* being 'driving forward' or 'to do with Áine'.

The ball used in hurling is a *sliotar*, which used to be made of the hair of cattle, the roots of gorse bushes or woven straw, like a large, dense seed, though it is now made of leather and cork. Michael Dames claims that the purpose of the game was 'to mime in the play the union between god and goddess, which determined the prosperity of the year to come'.[‡]

Does this mean that men played a ceremonial game around the time of Samhain in which they used penis-like accoutrements to beat the large seed around the land? Presumably the aim was to try hitting it into some specific orifice. This idea of the game being played

† Michael Dames, *Mythic Ireland* (London: Thames and Hudson, 1992; republished as *Ireland: A Sacred Journey* in 2000).
‡ Dames, *Mythic Ireland*.

by the gods is echoed in an account from 1945 by a local man, Thomas Ball, who told of a hurling match that took place between the fairies of Knockainy, led by Áine, and those at Knockfierna, led by the god Donn Fírinne, to decide who would produce the best crop of potatoes. The match was played cross-country, presumably with the pitch extending the full 25km between these sacred hills.[†] The folklorist Fionán Mac Coluim refers to similar matches between fairy groups in Co. Waterford and in Connacht to determine who got the crop of the year. Potatoes arrived in Ireland only in the late sixteenth century, but that doesn't mean that the story isn't far older than that particular detail.

We'll never truly understand the full extent of the roles played by the likes of Crom Dubh and Áine at a site like Lough Gur. Their heyday was long, long ago. That any lore has survived locally at all is due to the tendency among farmers to be superstitious and rather conservative when it comes to rituals related to the land. It's likely they just continued practising elements of their old beliefs for centuries after they had adopted Christianity. For all Jesus' talk of sowing and reaping, he wasn't a grain god like Crom Dubh, and if you abandoned the old deity who had ensured so many good harvests you risked provoking his ire. This is possibly why there are accounts of bull sacrifices happening in places like Cois Fharraige,

---

† Ball's account is given in Käte Müller-Lisowski, 'Contributions to a study in Irish folklore: Traditions about Donn', *Béaloideas*, Vol. 18, No. 1/2 (June–December 1948), pp 142–99.

Co. Galway, right up into the eighteenth century, and also in Loch Maree near the Isle of Skye in Scotland from the seventeenth century.[†]

For us today, our challenge is to try to pick out all the loose threads and remnants of lore that still linger in any spot of land and then combine this with visiting these places and walking the land, feeling what the land wants to tell us. Such subjective exploration will never be as precise as an archaeological excavation, and academics will often dismiss it, but if the land wants you to understand more about it, it will find ways to let you know.

<hr />

† Máire MacNeill, *Festival of Lughnasa: A Study of the Survival of the Celtic Festival of the Beginning of Harvest* ([London]: Oxford University Press, 1962).

FÓIDÍN MEARAÍ

The key message from Lough Gur is about the fractal nature of landscape in Ireland – how even seemingly insignificant sites can reveal a millefeuille of layers if we take the time to look around and do some research. There is culture, wisdom and lore lurking behind every rock, tree and mound.

After such an extensive consideration of the lake and its surroundings, I realise I have wandered a little bit astray. I'm now emerging back into the light, a bit disoriented and wondering how I got here. There's a term for this in Irish, *fóidín mearaí* (or *fóidín mearbhaill*). It refers to a patch of ground that looks no different from any other, but if you step on it you are catapulted into a different dimension. Things shift their parameters and turn topsy-turvy.

Fóidín means 'little sod of earth', occasionally one that has been kicked up in the air by wild dancing, and *mearaí* (or *mearbhaill*) means 'bewilderment', 'dizziness' or 'confusion'. Throughout the country there's a belief that the fairies put a spell on certain patches of land and that, if you happen to step on them, you'll lose your way and find it hard to regain your bearings until the fairies tire of their game and release you from the spell.

They're like snares set in the space-time continuum, and the effect can last for several hours, or even days. During this period, time is unaccounted for and familiar places look indecipherable. Occasionally, a person might hear their name called or see someone they thought they knew and follow them, only to be found some time later with no memory of how they came to be miles from where they should be. It's never a positive experience but there are ways of avoiding it. If you can remember to turn your coat inside out you can break the spell, but most of the time people don't remember this until later. Frank Maguire from Tullyback, Co. Cavan, explained in 1938:

> When a person is out at night and stands on
> such a sod, he goes astray and loses all idea of

direction, so that he wanders hopelessly around, generally until morning. Sometimes in his wanderings he may reach a road or house and then he is all right. It is helpful if such a thing happens to you to take off your coat and turn it inside out and wear it thus. That is the only hope of undoing the charm.[†]

Maguire went on to describe how a neighbour of his, Tom Dolan of Altateskin, 'stood on a stray sod one evening when he was searching for his cattle. The next evening he was wandering around Florencecourt some 14 miles away.' This happened in the 1920s. Maguire added, 'A very short time afterwards Dolan was taken to Monaghan Mental Hospital.'

In an interview recorded as part the Co. Wexford mapping project About This Place, you can watch John Murphy of Morriscastle recount how he stood on a 'stray sod' near Ballyscough Bridge in Macamore and immediately lost his way.[‡] Only when he turned his coat around could he find the way out of the field, but even then the fairies tried to force his car around and pull it back towards the errant sod.

The scholar Dáithí Ó hÓgáin pointed out that the 'combined mystical and menacing nature of lonely places

---

[†]   Schools' Collection, National Folklore Archive. https://www.duchas.ie/en/cbes/5044784.

[‡]   https://youtu.be/4he3fwIBlFA. Michael Fortune's web project About This Place (2013–16) is accessible at http://www.aboutthisplace.ie.

caused them often to be regarded with a degree of awe'.[†]
This in turn gave rise to phenomena such as the *fóidín mearaí* and the *féar gortach* ('hungry grass'), which was a patch of grass that would cause a ravenous hunger to descend on tired travellers, and also the *ceo draíochta* ('magic mist'), in which a sudden dark mist would descend, bringing with it fear, anxiety and often death.

These things often happened in remote areas of wild or liminal land, but there is also an account by a woman from Dunmore, Co. Galway, who claimed that there was a *fóidín mearaí* on the town square in Tuam, Co. Galway, and 'if a person stands on this with his foot in a certain position he is put astray'. She described how three men were going home one night from a wake in Carrowkeel:

> All felt they were going the right way. Two of them were turned back to the wake again. It was said it was the fóidin mearbhall that put them astray.[‡]

The *sean-nós* singer Seosamh Ó hÉanaí also speaks of how these alienating patches of earth can be near at hand. He tells of falling under the spell of *féar gortach* just twenty yards from his own front door. In the audio archives of Cartlanna Sheosaimh Uí Éanaí there's a recording of him explaining how he was going to a wake

---

† Dáithí Ó hÓgáin, *Irish Superstitions: Irish Spells, Old Wives' Tales and Folk Beliefs* (Dublin: Gill & Macmillan, 2002).
‡ Schools' Collection, National Folklore Archive. https://www.duchas.ie/en/cbes/4569057/4567642.

in a neighbour's house and forgot to put a pinch of salt on his tongue as protection before setting out, and so when he stood on a patch of ground where someone had died during the Famine, he immediately fell into a stupor and went astray for three whole days. 'People were looking for me and walking over me, but nobody could see me,' he explains. 'I could think, but I didn't know what to think. I couldn't see anybody and nobody could see me.'

Fortunately, Ó hÉanaí finally recalled the advice to turn his coat inside out, 'and that's what I did and then I knew what I was.' It's like Dorothy in *The Wizard of Oz* clicking her heels to get back to Kansas: she could have done it at any time, but it's about coming to the realisation that you have the power to do so – that we have the ability within ourselves to steer ourselves out of difficult situations and find the way home.

By all accounts, it's a most disconcerting experience, especially because, as Ó hÉanaí explains, people don't tend to believe you when you try to explain it. In some ways the phenomenon is less common now, though all of us have probably experienced a similar sensation, when using satnavs, of being lured around in circles by a disembodied voice that leads us ever further from our destination. We know there is a way to break the spell by turning off the app, but our disorientation can be such that we forget to do so. I've started to wonder if there might have been a *fóidín mearaí* beneath the flagstone in the house of the old man who first introduced me to the goddess Áine.

I certainly didn't mean to devote two weeks of my life to Áine and Crom Dubh, and the only reason I was able to do that was that my girlfriend suddenly fell under a trance of her own that felt as near to a fairy spell as any I can imagine. She was struck down with a bad bout of coronavirus disease, which led her through a mire of pain, fever and delirium that lasted a fortnight and made her seem like a totally different person. Her spirit seemed whisked away. Finally, as I write these words, she is beginning to come back to herself again, but now I've contracted the virus too, so I may be swept off to other places for a while myself.

UISNEACH:
THE NAVEL

O ur journey through the landscape is gradually
morphing into a Celtic knot of spiralling thread,
spreading out through the derivation of words, the
lineages of gods, the lore of place names and the mach-
inations of powerful dynasties. You might wonder what
could possibly unite such disparate elements.

Each aspect and location seems limitless, especially
considering how many of them extend back far through
time and into the infinity of the Otherworld. Yet there
is indeed a single unifying concept. It's to be found,

appropriately enough, near the very centre of Ireland. It's just a rock, in a way. Although that's like saying that the Black Stone in the Kaaba in Mecca is just a rock – or, for that matter, the Monolith in *2001: A Space Odyssey*.

The massive limestone boulder that I'm referring to was deposited on a hillside in what is now Co. Westmeath over twelve thousand years ago when the ice sheets were retreating at the end of the last ice age. It's four metres high and about thirty tonnes in weight, and it has been split and shaped into a dramatic form by eons of erosion. It's called Ail na Míreann ('Rock of Divisions'), or the Cat Stone, and according to a raft of folklore, mythology, archaeology and place name lore, it was not only the point at which all of Ireland was united but also the point through which it could communicate with realms beyond. Everything we have explored so far on our journey can be seen to spring from this centre point. It's an *axis mundi* around which all existence revolves.

That's a hard concept for us to accept today, as it relates to a way of seeing the world and experiencing reality that is mostly forgotten. And, of course, it's also hard to find historical evidence and rational accounts of beliefs that are beyond the rational. But if there is indeed a central plug of the matrix, a node from which all life emanates, expect to find it here, in a nondescript upland field on a hilly outcrop amid the boggy expanses of the midlands.

Again, as with Lough Gur, this is certainly not the dramatic landscape of the Skellig Islands or the Cliffs of Moher. No seminal scenes from *Star Wars* movies or *Game of Thrones* adventures will be filmed here. The midlands are as undramatic as midland regions tend to be, yet on a small and saucer-shaped island like Ireland, they have one advantage: they are relatively close to everywhere else, and even low hills can offer great views, as from the Hill of Ward in Co. Meath. From the summit of Uisneach, the hill on which Ail na Míreann stands, twenty out of the thirty-two counties of Ireland can be seen.

This helps explain why it was considered an important spot, but it's still surprising to learn that, from what we can decipher from pre-Christian mythology, Uisneach was regarded as the centre of the Irish firmament, just as the Tiantan Temple of Heaven in Beijing was by the people of the Ming and Qing dynasties. The belief that this was the point from which all life and energy radiated was made manifest each year in the form of a ritual fire that was lit on the summit.

This wasn't just any fire: it provided the seed flame that was used to light torches that were then carried to all the significant hilltops visible from Uisneach to light a further series of fires on them. Thus, a ring of fire was created surrounding the central sacred inferno. And from these outer fires it is believed that a further team of runners brought embers or oil torches out to form a second ring along the higher hilltops that surround much of the coastline. This was done so that, within a matter of hours, there would be beacon fires on every significant hill in Ireland, forming a massive sacred eye staring up into the heavens. Suddenly everything and everyone was visibly united – all seeded from a single spark, lit at Uisneach.

It's a dramatic concept, but how do we know whether it is true? Well, in the Dinnseanchas there's an account of Mide (chief seer of the people of Nemed and foster son of the goddess Ériu) lighting the first fire in Ireland, 'and the fire spread throughout the whole of Erin, and for seven years was it ablaze. And from that fire were kindled every chief fire and every chief hearth in Ireland.'

Mide was then dwelling on the hill at Uisneach, from where he exacted punishment on seers who disapproved of his fire ritual by cutting 'the tongues out of the heads of the druids, and took them with him, and buried them under him in the ground of Uisneach'. In subsequent centuries Uisneach became known in lore as the centre of the festival of Bealtaine, an annual fire festival held at the beginning of May to cleanse people's homes, spirits, souls and animals after the long dark winter and also to spark the land into life again. The *mórdáil Uisnig* ('large assembly of Uisneach') is an event often cited in mythology. The name Uisneach derives from the Proto-Celtic word for 'hearth' or 'temple', according to T.F. O'Rahilly.

In the ninth century, Bishop Cormac mac Cuileannáin described the Bealtaine ritual as consisting of 'two fires which Druids used to make with great incantations, and they used to bring the cattle [as a safeguard] against the diseases of each year to those fires. They used to drive the cattle between them.'

In the seventeenth century the historian Geoffrey Keating recorded that Bealtaine was indeed the major event at Uisneach. People would gather

> to exchange with one another their goods, their wares and their valuables. They also used to offer sacrifices to the chief god they adored ... and it was their wont to light two fires ... in every district in Ireland and to drive a weakling of each species [of] cattle between the two fires as a preservative to shield them from all the disease that year.

In the eighteenth century the philosopher John Toland, who was born Seán Ó Tuathaláin on the Inishowen Peninsula, Co. Donegal, recalled a hilltop fire site close to Derry that was simply known as Bealtaine. He describes a series of fire-beacon sites being lit on May Eve, for the Bealtaine festival, 'which being in sight of some other, could not but afford a glorious show over a whole nation'. However, it's not clear whether Toland witnessed this or simply read about it.

But right up into the twentieth century there was a folk tradition regarding the sacred fires of Bealtaine, through which people drove their cattle and from which they carried embers to significant points around their homes to protect cattle and property. And while the origin of the name Bealtaine is disputed, most linguists agree that the second syllable derives from the Irish word for fire, *tine*.

The idea of a central fire that then radiates out in the form of satellite fires is familiar as a central motif in the story of St Patrick, as it was vital on his arrival in Ireland that he break the tradition of fire and sun worship that had taken root to achieve his goal of Christianising the pagans. So, just a year after his arrival in AD 433, he travelled to the Hill of Slane in the days before the Bealtaine festival and lit a fire there in defiance of the pagan high king Lóegaire, who had ordered that no fire be lit at the time of Bealtaine before the ceremonial one at Tara was lit from a flame brought from Uisneach.

Slane is the closest significant high point to the Hill of Tara, but historians and archaeologists now surmise that Patrick may have lit his fire on a different hill, possibly one visible from Uisneach. Either way, he purposely went to a hilltop of pagan worship to break the tradition of a prominent king or druid lighting the first ceremonial fire.

It was vital that he did this, because the lighting of a bonfire on the Hill of Uisneach, and the spreading of that fire to the Hill of Tara and then on to prominent sites throughout Ireland, was the annual catalyst for the rebirth of the goddess and her domain of nature. How long the tradition stretches back is impossible to say, but the radiating circles and the symbols resembling wheel spokes, known as 'fire eyes', carved on megaliths at ceremonial sites on hilltops from six thousand years ago seem remarkably reminiscent of rings of fire encircling a central ritual blaze.

TEMPLE AND STONE

It is clear that the Hill of Uisneach was a prominent point that was marked with ritual fires for thousands of years, but why was the centre so important? To understand this, we need to turn back to something Fintan mac Bóchra said. You'll recall that he told the giant bearing the 'triple key' who seeded Ireland with sacred trees that Ireland was divided into five provinces called *cúigí* ('fifths'). It is still divided into *cúigí* but there are now only four of them: the provinces Ulster, Leinster, Munster and Connacht. It seems the fifth province was as much a concept as a place, and we've since lost the ability to conceive of this notion. It was known as Midhe ('middle') and was supposedly the core that connected all the other provinces.

Midhe was the centre of kingship but also the navel through which this reality was connected with the realms above, below and beyond. It was as much an interdimensional province as a geographical one. The only remnant of it is in the names of the counties Meath and Westmeath, which in Irish are Contae na Mí and Contae na hIarmhí, *mí* being the modern spelling of *midhe*. Co. Meath is still known as the Royal County, as it was the seat of high kingship from the Iron Age onwards. It was a royal centre of sacred governance, the nexus of all life.

That this centre was regarded as an umbilical point is hinted at in a line from the fourteenth-century manuscript Leabhar Buidhe Leacáin ('Yellow Book of Lecan') about the birth of Fintan mac Bóchra. Fintan's patronymic, mac Bóchra, means 'son of the ocean', from the Old Irish word *bóchna* ('sea' or 'ocean'). He was said to be the sole Irish survivor of the Great Flood and so was born from the amniotic waters of the sea. On returning to Uisneach eons later, he said, 'It is long since I drank a drink of the deluge over the navel of Uisneach,' implying that Ail na Míreann ('Rock of Divisions') was a form of umbilicus that facilitated his birth into this world from the magic realms beyond.

All activities, mythology, rituals and ceremonies centred on the fissured and fragmented limestone boulder Ail na Míreann, which nature has shaped into a massive orb that is splitting open under the impact of elemental forces over time. But there are other ancient remains on the hill. On first glance it may seem like a bland stretch of rolling pasture, but in fact there are more than forty archaeological monuments here, mostly ritual and funerary sites, including burial monuments and enclosures, standing stones, ring forts, barrows, holy wells and an embanked roadway.

Most of these are now beneath the ground, and all are rather muted and covered in lush nitrogen-enriched rye grass, so you really need someone to decipher the site for you, or else to read the archaeological reports in advance. Fortunately, there are regular tours led by passionate and well-informed local guides who dramatically summon the past alive from the somnambulant cattle-grazed hills.

The earliest monument on Uisneach is a passage tomb near the summit dating back about five thousand years to the Neolithic era, though it's now just a heap of stones covered in grass with signs of a portal facing the setting sun and a large enclosure encircling it. It's known as St Patrick's Bed, tying in with a story about how Patrick spent time here in his efforts to Christianise Ireland.

The most extensive remains are an Iron Age ring fort that was excavated in the 1920s. Legend has it that

TEMPLE AND STONE

it is the palace of King Tuathal Techtmar from the first century AD, and archaeologists agree that it was most likely a royal site at about that time. Numerous ash-lined pits were discovered that appear to have been used for sacred fires involving animal sacrifice. Beside them are large flat stones that archaeologists surmise may have been pulled over the flames to rapidly quench them as part of the ritual. There was also a large ash bed containing thoroughly charred animal skeletons that Roseanne Schot, lead investigator on the Tara Research Project, believes is consistent with a sanctuary site in which fire was kept burning perpetually, or kindled at frequent intervals.

There are other remains among the palace ruins that were built much later by one of Ireland's most powerful medieval tribes, Clann Cholmáin, who were part of the southern Uí Néill dynasty and were known as the kings of Uisneach. They were also the kings of Meath on and off between the eighth and early eleventh centuries. Since kingship in Ireland relied for its legitimacy on establishing a direct lineage with the great ancestral leaders, both real and mythological, it's no surprise that they used Uisneach as their centre of royal power.

This was the hill on which Dagda, the chief deity of the magical race Tuatha Dé Danann, was believed to have lived. On its north side are two underground chambers that were said to be the stables where he kept his divine solar horses that pulled the sun through the sky. The great god associated with light and art, Lugh, came here to rescue his mother from the tyranny of the evil Fomorians and their leader, Balor of the Evil Eye (who is also equated with the scorching sun).

Lugh later drowned here in a lake on the hill that is still known as Lough Lugh, and he's said to be buried beneath a nearby mound, Carn Lughdach. Even the principal queen of Tuatha Dé Danann, Ériu, is said to be buried here, right under Ail na Míreann. That she was stationed here, right at what was believed to be the sacred centre point of Ireland, is a factor in her being adopted by the Gaelic people as one of their own goddesses, and she even gave Ireland its name, Ériu, later Éire, which the Vikings altered to 'Ériu's Land', giving rise to 'Ireland'.

But as we saw with the fire beacons, the real power of Uisneach is not so much with the site itself as with its role as a node from which everything else is visible, fuelled and energised. The presence of Lugh, Dagda and his solar horses, the god Balor and the archaeological remnants of fire rituals all point to this being a significant sun-oriented site.

Its solar orientation is further strengthened by Uisneach's connection with the Bealtaine festival on 1 May, when even into living memory farmers and leaders would gather at the beginning of the growing season each year for a ritual of rejuvenation, sparking the land into fertility by means of sacred bonfires that then spread out from the centre to all points throughout Ireland. It was natural that such powers would emanate from the core and that people would make annual pilgrimage to the region to invoke and ignite these powers.

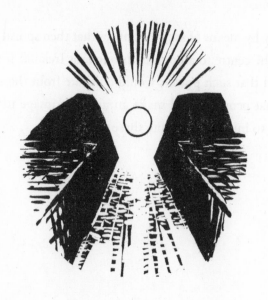

SUN LINES

When exploring Lough Gur we looked at the remarkable sun alignments visible within the stone circle, bearing in mind that solar alignments are not an exact science and that almost any two points can be made to align with the sun depending on one's vantage point. Nevertheless, there are some remarkable meridian lines and geometrical connections with the sun that can be traced from Uisneach.

Anthony Murphy on his site mythicalireland.com has shown a direct line from Ail na Míreann on Uisneach north towards the megalithic complex at Loughcrew and onwards to Slieve Gullion in Co. Armagh. Any two points can be made to align with the sun, but finding a third point on the line that is closely associated with the other two points shows either conscious intent or a remarkable coincidence. The alignment is clearly visible to anyone who cares to check on the Google Earth app, which factors in the curvature of the planet to allow for accurate calculation of sightlines. Sunrise on the summer solstice follows this line, and what is truly surprising is how accurately the line intersects the centre of the passage temple inside the most important rock mound on the summit of Loughcrew (Cairn T).

Somehow the Neolithic builders of the Loughcrew cairns and of the cairn known as Calliagh Berra's House on Slieve Gullion managed to position these buildings so as to be directly in alignment at sunrise on the summer solstice, and also at sunset on the winter solstice, from the opposite direction. There's more than one hundred kilometres between the Hill of Uisneach and Slieve Gullion, and the buildings on Loughcrew and Slieve Gullion were built more than five thousand years ago.

This would be remarkable in itself, but what really gives me goosebumps is that because Ail na Míreann is on the south-western slope of the Hill of Uisneach, while Loughcrew and Slieve Gullion are to the north-east, the sites are not directly visible by a sightline but are connected by a linear alignment. For the direct sightline one must walk up three hundred metres to the summit of Uisneach. Our forebears must have had some uncanny ways of plotting and mapping their surroundings in complex ways.

On the hills at Loughcrew (Sliabh na Caillí) in Co. Meath, circular rock cairns were built five thousand years ago with stone-lined passages that lead into womb-like sanctuaries. These were decorated with spiral carvings that form a dizzyingly complex geometrical pattern of concentric circles. There were linear access routes between and within these circular cairns and their circular decorations that formed a further array of geometrical shapes. On top of all this convoluted geometrical entanglement, there is a further interrelationship between the solar alignments that intersect through radial lines with the circular stone of Ail na Míreann and the circular fires and circular ritual buildings that surround it on the Hill of Uisneach.

The *cailleach* gave Loughcrew its name. Sliabh na Caillí means 'hill of the witch', or 'hill of the wise woman' or 'hill of the veiled woman', and the *cailleach* in question is probably the pre-eminent goddess of the land, Cailleach Bhéarra, who was a deity connected with the destructiveness and bleakness of winter but also the rebirth and transformation that follow it. She is believed, in some lore, to have created the earth or at least to have been present for its creation. It's unlikely to be a coincidence that the ritual temple or cairn on Slieve Gullion is also called Calliagh Berra's House.

It was long known that by looking south from Calliagh Berra's House you could see the sun setting directly behind Loughcrew at the winter solstice. In fact, from Slieve Gullion the sun appears to consume the two dominant mammary-like hills of Loughcrew and their stone cairn nipples. Despite being more than sixty kilometres apart, they are entwined through the same goddess.

That the stone mounds resemble breasts may also be no coincidence. It has long been suggested that the entranceways to passage tombs (more accurately referred to as ritual temples, as archaeologists have found little evidence of entombment within them) represent vaginas into which the shaft of the male sun enters at dawn on significant days in the astral calendar. The sun sends its seeds through the birthing canal to fertilise the womb.

Michael Dames has argued that the principal cairn on Loughcrew represents the body of a divine female.[†] The ritual chamber within the mound represents her torso, with a belly and womb at the very centre and with smaller side chambers representing her two arms and her head. Inside the two principal cairns on Loughcrew, the chamber corresponding to the goddess's head has the most complex geometrical designs, including an array of 'fire rings' or 'sun eyes'.

At Cairn T, right outside the entranceway into the passageway, is a massive carved and decorated throne-

† Michael Dames, *Mythic Ireland* (London: Thames and Hudson, 1992; republished as *Ireland: A Sacred Journey* in 2000).

shaped limestone boulder that was once surrounded entirely with white quartz. It is known as the Hag's Chair – again seemingly a reference to Cailleach Bhéarra. The throne casts a further remarkable light on the idea of alignments. As well as being oriented towards the Pole Star, it also allows a person sitting in it to see both the Hill of Uisneach to the south-west and Slieve Gullion to the north-east. Thus, the throne becomes a unifying node connecting the two *cailleach* sites back to the umbilical centre of Ireland and, from there, out into unknowable realms towards the Pole Star in orbit 323 light years beyond our solar system.

Dames documents numerous other alignments with Uisneach, such as the direct line heading south to the goddess Áine's residence at Knockainy near Lough Gur in Co. Limerick, and the same line running north to the ritual and tribal centre of Late Bronze Age and Iron Age Ulster, Emain Macha (Navan Fort) in Co. Armagh. Sure enough, if these points are plotted on Google Maps and the earth's curvature is taken into account, they too reveal a perfect alignment over a distance of 239km. It's hard to understand how such alignments were ever created over such vast distances. In Irish we'd say, *Cuirfeadh sé meascán mearaí ort* (*meascán mearaí* meaning a mystification of mind, or going astray in other dimensions).

That Uisneach might be linked with Knockainy was hinted at earlier in the accounts of the two gods from Uisneach – Uainide and Eogabal – who laid claim to Knockainy and Lough Gur from their position in the navel centre of Ireland. But the fact that Knockainy, home of the goddess Áine, would be in direct alignment with the central location attributed to the god Macha at Emain Macha over two hundred kilometres to the north is just remarkable, especially as that line runs through the fulcrum point of Uisneach and also happens to pass through another important pre-Christian site, the summit of Slieve Felim (Sliabh Eibhlinne) in Co. Tipperary, where the goddess Fodla resided.

What should we make of all this? Is it pure coincidence, and if not, how were such complex astronomical and engineering feats achieved? These are mostly natural geographical features, with the exception of Emain Macha, which consists of a large circular hilltop enclosure built in the eighth century BC on a site that was occupied for thousands of years before that. Were the hills chosen for their alignments and then temples, tombs and ritual sites built on top of them, in the precise location that would align with surrounding sacred sites, as well as with the sun, moon or significant stars?

It seems that the land was like a game board or a four-dimensional matrix of significant energy points and that, over thousands of years, a series of ceremonial sites was constructed on these points, with a multilayered mythology developed to encompass them all. The stories and the stone structures are therefore secondary to the sites themselves. It is in the land that the power and the meaning reside. The land is a she, and she is a goddess. She is connected with everything, and her umbilicus is at Ail na Míreann on the Hill of Uisneach.

I can write that sentence easily enough, but for me to fully comprehend it is another matter. That Ail na Míreann could be a portal for the primal energy or sacred life force that infuses land, water, sea and sky – and that animates our lives – is just hard for our rational minds to accept. And yet for centuries the Hill of Uisneach maintained its allure as a place of power associated with rejuvenation and replenishment by people all over Ireland and even further afield. According to the historian Ruth Illingworth, 'Persian and other faraway traders were among those merchants who attended the Uisneach Lúnasa fair. It was even mentioned in the writings of Caesar.' A coin minted in Herat, Afghanistan, about 900 BC was found in a lake nearby.

For eons Uisneach has been a place to journey to at Bealtaine to gather energy for the season ahead, or else to visit at the time of the Lúnasa festival to celebrate the harvest. It's a virtually continuous tradition that lapsed for only a few decades in the past century under the pressure of colonial oppression. It's hard to underestimate the importance of this, and the fact that we feel so disconnected from it now shows how far we've drifted from our core.

This was not always the case. In 1919, during the War of Independence, Éamon de Valera addressed a Sinn Féin rally on the hill. Almost twenty years before, the organisation spearheading a recovery of Irish language and culture, Conradh na Gaeilge, held an annual *feis*, or gathering, there each August. A thousand years before that, Brian Boru, the *ard-rí*, came to Uisneach to lay claim to his sovereignty over Mide (Meath), when he finally managed to defeat the all-powerful Uí Néill, kings of Tara.

Even St Patrick, who had so bravely gone up against the *ard-rí* at Tara, didn't dare oppose Ail na Míreann directly. On his proselytising visit to Uisneach he was confronted by two local brothers who objected to his plan to build a church there as a sign of his dominance. Outraged by their audacity, he was about to curse them and the stones of Uisneach that they worshipped, but according to Bishop Tírechán, who wrote Patrick's biography in the seventh century, he was stopped in his tracks by his disciple Senchall. Patrick managed to get only the words 'A curse –' out of his mouth before Senchall quickly interjected, '– be on the stones of Uisneach.'

Tírechán was careful not to suggest that Patrick had directly cursed the most powerful pagan site himself. Instead, he limply agreed with Senchall, saying, 'Be it so.'

Michael Dames points to further alignments between Uisneach and the Hill of Ward at sunset in late November, as well as at the Samhain moon. There are also alignments with Croghan Hill, Co. Offaly, and with the Hill of Allen, Co. Kildare, which was the sacred seat of the Leinster kings until the eighth century. Naturally, there was also an alignment with Slievenamon (literally 'Mountain of the Women'), a domineering, mythologically rich dome that rises from the plain of south Co. Tipperary, and with Ard Éireann ('Height of Ireland'), the highest peak in the Slieve Bloom mountains, which continued to be an important place of pilgrimage till 1940. There was also, of course, an alignment with Rathcroghan and almost every other significant sacred site in Ireland.

It may take a long time before we can appreciate the full significance of these things. It requires us to radically reappraise our understanding of the world around us and our relationship to it. These connections, alignments and interrelations speak to an entirely different way of being in the world, possibly closer to the Asian system of meridian lines than to anything that survives in the West. Alternatively, the answers may lie within the complex spiral geometry of what is known as 'Celtic design' but that is far older than the Celts. The traditional Celtic knot motif that you see on stone carvings and souvenirs, and in the pages of illuminated manuscripts like the Book of Kells, is a profound representation of four-dimensional space that has yet to be fully explored.

I don't understand any of these things fully yet, but I'm curious and eager to learn more.

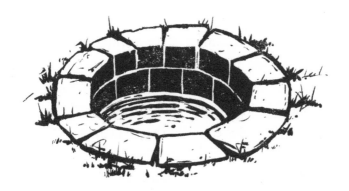

HOLY WELLS

The interconnection between this world and realms beyond seems to be represented by the infinite loop of the Celtic knot and is perhaps best manifested in the landscape in the form of holy wells. These sacred aqueous portals that rise from the depths of the earth appear to allow access to the Otherworld in a more direct way than other elements such as passage tombs, ring forts or even churches. There are hundreds and even thousands of sacred water sources in Ireland that have long been regarded as bridges connecting humans with a realm beyond the physical and rational. They are sanctuaries within the landscape, threshold sites that for centuries, and even millennia, allowed us to step back from the hullaballoo of daily existence and gain access to something grander and otherworldly – something infinite and unknown.

At one time almost every townland had a water source that was marked out for special devotion – a source of cures or solace in difficult times. Each was allied to a particular god or goddess, saint or mythical creature. It is a testament to their allure that so many survive today despite all the machine-churned turmoil of the twentieth century. The first thing to realise is that a well can take on many forms beyond the typical, stone-lined pool of clear water. They can be anything from tiny streams rising from a rock to bubbles emerging from the gravel of a riverbed or a muddy drinking pool for cattle or water gushing up through the sandy shore.

Many holy wells are in areas of spectacular beauty, often in groves of trees, in hollows in the landscape, at the edge of waysides or at liminal points where borders and boundaries meet. Others are hidden in the darkness of underground tunnels, chambers or caves, and others again are at the edge of the sea, where the salt water mixes with the fresh water twice daily. There are even some wells that consist of a measure of rain water held in an indentation of a solid rock. Their variance and mutability make it clear that they are as much a product of the subconscious and instinctive self as they are of the rational and practical mind.

The first question that needs to be asked, though, is why are they holy? Why are some wells regarded as sacred portals of divine energy or the eyes of God, and others just as utilitarian water sources that can be exploited and sullied with impunity? From an empirical standpoint, holy wells are no different from any other natural water source; in fact, any source of fresh spring water on the surface of the earth (or in caves or under the sea) can become a focus of devotion and thus be labelled holy.

So, how and why does it happen? That remains something of a mystery. Even gauging how long a well has been deemed holy is complicated. There are references in old manuscripts to pilgrims going to particular wells 1,500 years ago that still attract devoted visitors to this day. These wells may have been luring people to them for thousands of years before that. We can only really be sure of what has been documented since the advent of writing in Ireland in the fifth century.

There are other wells that appear to have risen to prominence within the last century. Perhaps more will come, although it is fair to assume that no water source has been newly deemed holy since about the 1970s and maybe even since electricity was extended throughout the island in the 1950s. That said, forgotten and abandoned wells are frequently being rediscovered and rejuvenated, so the number of wells is growing, not diminishing.

That these wells exerted such a strong influence on the people for so long hints at the power they contain. And whether their allure comes from the water itself or from the location, or from some complex energetic phenomenon, or maybe even from a more complex combination of all these primary elements of water, rock, soil, light and energy interacting in a specific way, is hard to gauge; but wells are ultimately about faith combining with elemental forces, and faith is not about reason but beyond it.

We must accept that the human attraction to wells, other than as mere sources of hydration and irrigation, is an unquantifiable factor, really discernible only to the well-goers themselves. You visit your local well because your parents and grandparents did so before you. Wells have always been places of private reflection, and occasionally of communal gathering, as on the 'patron' or 'pattern' day that is associated with many wells and is a catalyst for a large gathering in the community. It is believed that on these days, and often at a specific hour of the day, the well reaches its peak potency. Often this corresponds to the threshold hour of dawn or midnight. At this time the magical beast or goddess or saint associated with the well becomes more accessible and tangible. Often it takes on the form of a magical trout or salmon, or an eel.

Many wells are thought by some to cure specific ailments. Those that are still visited regularly in the present day are thought to offer a cure for ailments that conventional medicine finds hard to tackle. These healing properties have been believed in for generations, and the stories that are told of past cures perpetuate such beliefs. Even if the beliefs are no longer being passed down within families, there are always a few stalwarts in each community keen to broadcast the news far and wide. Listen to any radio phone-in show when they're discussing how to get rid of warts or a sty in the eye, and you'll hear callers eager to boast of the efficacy of their local well.

There's only so much one can convey about these multidimensional spaces. A visit is necessary to get a true sense of them. The first thing you'll notice is that most wells have not been abandoned and that many still attract a continual stream of people who turn up in ones and twos throughout the day. You need to linger a while to fully appreciate the intangible, otherworldly atmosphere these places can have.

Watching how others interact with the site will teach you the characteristics of each well. Many of them require a choreography of ritualistic movement to unlock their full power. Visitors may perform a series of sequential movements, often interacting with a specific sacred stone or venerable tree before approaching the most sanctified area of the well.

The ritual often involves the circumambulation of the well or a nearby tree or stone, or a combination of all these things, and the reciting of prayers aloud or in silence. There is often a necessity to touch, stroke, kiss or scrape a rock, tree or body of water as part of these movements. It appears to be a gesture to acknowledge, and show deference to, the elemental forces in these things.

These days the choreographic code of movement and words needed to unlock the potency of a well is often written on a signboard, but previously such actions would have been known only to the local community and chosen initiates. Likewise, the saint, serpent or goddess connected with the well is often a local character that might not be known about even a few valleys away.

It should be stressed that none of these elements is unique to Ireland. The practices of visiting wells and walking sunwise around them, or catching sight of a magical fish in them, or using them as psychological aids, or showing deference to sacred stones and trees in the vicinity, are also to be found in South Africa, Japan, Russia, Brazil and many other places. They are universal practices, as is the idea that the well is protected by a magic fish, sacred eel, crocodile or python.

Of course, these ideas, like so much of well lore and tradition, are at odds with Christianity, which is one reason the Church disapproved so strongly of worshipping wells that hadn't been thoroughly Christianised. Ever since the Reformation, in particular, efforts were made to stamp out well worshipping. Communal devotion was to be restricted to Church property, where the priest could oversee it. In 1704 the Irish Parliament imposed a penalty of a whipping or a fine of ten shillings on those who assembled at wells. Church leaders branded those who frequented them as superstitious and idolatrous, but the popularity of water sources continued. The pagan belief in the power of sites that contained a water source, often in the company of a significant rock and tree, held strong.

Not only were all the past cures proof of their enduring power, but communities recognised that there were psychological benefits too to having a sanctuary space at which psychosomatic conditions could be alleviated. A trip to the well was believed to help reduce anxiety and offer hope of a cure for a problem that was causing worry. The efficacy of this can be still seen today in the number of votive offerings left behind by visitors in the belief that a totem symbol of their ailment or the source of their anxiety will help in the cure. One finds buttons, brooches, toys, baby soothers, crosses, medals, scapulars, coins, fragments of rosary beads, nails, screws, pins and a variety of clooties, which are scraps of frayed clothing or bandages. It is believed that as these clooties rot away, so too will the ailment or cause of concern.

The well provided a respite, a place of calm where one could reflect on and reappraise matters beyond the busyness of home. That said, wells weren't always sanctuaries of tranquillity. On their pattern day, or saint's day, they could become as wild and rambunctious as a modern music festival, especially in the past few centuries. Pilgrims would flock from miles around to dutifully perform the rituals associated with the site – normally a series of Aves (Hail Marys), Paters (Our Fathers) and Glorias (Glory Bes) – while circling the well and the other sacred rocks or trees connected with it. Once this was completed, they would hurriedly join the feasting and cavorting, which involved scenes of wrestling, dancing, boxing, courting, hurling, horse racing, feasting and drinking, according to numerous eighteenth and nineteenth-century accounts. So, on one day a year, the placid spot would reveal its shadow side, as it was transmuted into a chaotic melee of gluttony, revelry and merriment.

Finally, and perhaps most significantly, it's worth bearing in mind the realisation that is emerging on this journey: of the essential feminine nature of the Irish landscape. While many of the wells are now associated with a male saint, most would probably have been associated with female divine energy in pre-Christian times. The Church made no secret of the fact that many wells were originally sites of pagan worship.

In fact, the Lives of the Saints are full of accounts of St Patrick, St Colm Cille, St Brigid and lesser saints going around 'saining' wells, which involved their tracking down and ambushing pagan groups worshipping at water sites and then using their God-ordained power, or more likely their political influence, to banish the well guardian or the seer who was leading the ritual. They would then kill off the magic serpent, demon or other Otherworldly beast that guarded it, proceeding to 'sain' the well by blessing it. The 'purified' water was then used to baptise the pagan onlookers who had watched this display of power and would be swayed into converting to this new and dramatic all-conquering faith.

And while it seems to have been male druidic priests who oversaw the wells, the water sources themselves were regarded as entrances to the mysterious female realm of life creation and nourishment. It is not far-fetched to imagine them as representative of vaginal portals into the womb of the mother goddess.

Our old system of belief had, if nothing else, a remarkable ability to encompass all aspects of human life and existence. That so many of these timeless portals to our past and the natural world still exist in the landscape is of immense value to us all. We owe it to ourselves and our ancestors to keep them animated and vibrant for generations to come. In return, at the very least, they will continue to offer us life-giving water as well as isolated havens of peace and contemplation.

BOGLAND

If wells are liminal, peripheral spaces in the landscape, bogs are similar but on a grander scale. These heathery, sodden realms of olive, emerald, umber, ochre, bronze and the brownest of purples have been places of mystery and intrigue in Ireland. During the course of their millennia-long existence, they remained isolated and apart from human civilisation until we finally found a way to exploit them for profit on an industrial scale after the First World War, when advances in continuous-track technology allowed tanks and heavy machinery to traverse soft ground with less likelihood of sinking. The technology was soon honed to create monstrous mechanical contraptions that could roll lightly over quaking bog, scooping up vast stretches of the soft peat and extruding it into compact bricks. Once these monsters were set loose on the bogs, much of the mystery and magic of these richly pigmented swathes of rusted bracken and spongy sphagnum was robbed. They became places of commerce and profit.

A Neolithic farmer returning to Ireland in the early twentieth century would have found the landscape entirely altered, apart from some of our waterways and the bogs that still shimmered white with bog cotton in summer and that glowed in burnished reds and russets in autumn. These had always been respected as places apart, right up to the 1930s, when the Turf Development Board was set up, with my cousin Aodogán O'Rahilly as a board member and, later, chairperson. With ruthless efficiency he and his team began the wholesale industrialisation of this precious environmental resource that had gradually built up over thousands of years. They began to pulverise and haul out this once biodiverse and sacred landscape. In time, the Turf Development Board became Bord na Móna, and their technical prowess kept improving, so that over the past fifty years a quarter of our remaining raised bogs were wiped out.

Of the original 300,000 hectares of raised bog in Ireland, 24 per cent was lost to mechanical extraction and 2 per cent to forestry, and a staggering 64 per cent was lost to small-scale turf-cutting by families or local contractors. Back in 2009 the Irish Peatland Conservation Council estimated that only 10 per cent of raised bog was still intact and worthy of conservation, and this figure may have dropped since.

The other type of bogland in Ireland is blanket bog, found more in upland areas in the west. Of the 770,000 hectares of blanket bog that once existed here, only 28 per cent survives. Turf-cutting caused the loss of a third of it, and another third was destroyed by over-grazing and the planting of conifer forests through it.

We are only now beginning to acknowledge all that has been lost. There are more than twenty carnivorous plant species that rely on peatland and many of these offer valuable medicinal compounds for treating ailments such as catarrh. There are exotic-looking lichens and the many forms of sphagnum moss that are found only on bogs and that have remarkable abilities to soak up liquid and release penicillin-like chemicals. There are also the various cures associated with medicinal peatland plants, such as bog rosemary, bog cotton, bog myrtle, ling heather, heaths, crowberry, cranberry, bilberry and purple moor grass. And there are the endangered bog birds, including curlews, red grouse, golden plovers, grey partridges and meadow pipits.

We are at a tipping point when it comes to our bogs. Despite the remarkable destructive ability of both our domestic turf-cutters and the massive mechanical extractors, Ireland still manages to be a superpower in peatland. After Canada and Finland, we have the most surviving peatland. We possess 8 per cent of the world's remaining blanket bog. We also have the finest surviving examples of raised bogs, as well as half of all the intact oceanic raised bog systems left in Europe. Ireland even gave the word 'bog' to the world: it derives from *bogach* ('soft').

Sixteen per cent of this island is covered by these precious ecosystems that are some of the oldest natural habitats on earth and once covered vast swathes of the planet. They are as varied and biodiverse as any rainforest and could vastly enhance our lives in myriad ways, if only we were to move away from our exploitative attitude and the subconscious fear that lingers inside many of us.

One of the prime reasons that bogs have survived untouched for so long is this often unacknowledged wariness we have about them. For thousands of years they've been regarded as eerie quagmires of unsteady ground, as places to be avoided. A landscape that is neither fully solid nor liquid cannot be trusted, especially one that has already swallowed up many people. Ask any bogland community and they will tell you of people who have been taken by the bog. There's even a popular curse, *Breith i bpoll móna ort* ('May you get caught in a bog hole').

Some have within them deep, perilous pits that have been covered over by a false floor of grasses and moss and that can swallow you whole if you step on them. And there is no easy escape once you're in: the more you struggle, the more slippery and crumbly the sides become and the less likely it is you'll get out. You soon learn to just give in and wait, hoping that someone might happen along through whatever isolated stretch of expanse you happen to be and that they can find a rope or branch to throw to you. If not, you just wait as the bog water seeps deep into you and hypothermia sets in.

The writer Kerri ní Dochartaigh has shared with me her own recent experience of climbing into a bog ditch in wellingtons to retrieve her dog and realising that her feet had been sucked under and that she was slowly sinking. She was aware that struggling would only bring her deeper, and after a time a calmness came over her, which allowed her to notice how all of life – the insects, butterflies and birds – was continuing on obliviously, or maybe accepting her plight with respect and honour. She was in the process of feeding the bog, as so many people, animals and things have done before her, sinking down into it to be leached of precious nutrients and then preserved for ever in a partially desiccated form.

Her calmness freed her mind and allowed her to remember that she had a multitool penknife in a pocket of her work coat. Fortunately, it was in an upper pocket, as she would not have been able to reach her trouser pocket. She was able to use the tool to hook onto a root and pull herself out.

Ní Dochartaigh is not the only person I've known to fall foul of bogs, and they all tell me what a chilling experience it is to find oneself suddenly helpless in a wet living grave. It's for good reason that these isolated, lonely places were avoided – other than by ne'er-do-wells who needed to secretly dump unwanted things or commit nefarious acts.

Peatlands are obviously most dangerous at night when the pits that have been dug in them (to extract turf, to ret flax and other fibrous plants or to preserve things, or possibly even as bathing pools for therapeutic uses) are not visible. It was widely believed that malevolent spirits would try to lure you to your death by beckoning with ghost lanterns and beacons that were often seen moving across the bog in the distance, as though they were being carried by people guiding you to safety. My father saw them in Killashee Bog in Co. Longford when he was a boy in the 1920s. This was the *tine ghealáin* or *Liam na Sopóige* – frightening illuminations appearing out of the eerie blackness that were thought to be lost souls condemned to wander perpetually through the black wilderness.

The principal bog story is about Seán na Gealaí ('Seán of the Moon', or 'jack o' lantern'), who manages to renege on a deal with the Devil by tricking him a series of times. When Seán eventually dies, having avoided the Devil's attempts to snare him throughout his life, he is refused entry to both Heaven and Hell and is condemned to roam the wilderness with a single burning ember taken from the fires of Hell. It is this you see flickering from a carved-out turnip in the bog at night.

Seán na Gealaí formed the basis for the first major work of modern literature in Irish, *Séadna* (1904), by Fr Peadar Ua Laoghaire. Similar stories are to be found in boggy areas all round the world. In Brazil the spirit is known as Boi-tata ('fiery serpent'), in Bangladesh it's the Aleya ('marsh ghost light'), on the Mekong River in Thailand they are called Naga fireballs and in Norway it's the Hessdalen light.

The scientific explanation is that the lights are formed by the spontaneous combustion of phosphines and methane that arise from the bog through organic decay, or else it's a form of bioluminescent fungus or algae specific to that environment. Either way, they've helped add to the sense that bogs are eerie, half-drowned realms, stalked by ghosts, grotesques and vengeful characters best avoided.

PEAT POLLEN

B ogs are stalked by ghosts but not necessarily by evil ones. Rather, they have within them the mummified remnants and energetic residues of almost everything that ever happened there long ago. If land can be regarded as a memory bank, then bogs are its cerebellum, diligently recording every scattered pollen spore and drowned beetle, every fallen tree and wet winter.

The sediment of the previous year's decomposition is preserved year after year in the fibrous sponge of peat, so that over hundreds and thousands of years, as layer upon layer of peat accumulates, a memory bank several metres high is built up. You can look on bogs as nature's archivists, laden with ghost memories of past landscapes.

And within that condensed matting of organic matter there is information in clearly defined strata about the amount of rainfall and evaporation in a particular decade. Remembered within the bog are the plants and forest cover that surrounded it, the insects that depended on it, the depth of the water table and the ferocity of the winter storms.

There are two forms of bog – blanket bog and raised bog – and both offer insights into the past. Blanket bog is found in areas of high rainfall, mostly in the west and in mountainous areas, while raised bogs are largely confined to the midlands and other low-lying areas. Blanket bog was created as a direct result of human interference thousands of years ago, when our Neolithic forebears began clearing the hilltops to create grazing and growing land. At least that's what some environmental biologists believe; others say it was shifting weather patterns that led to its development.

According to the hilltop-clearing argument, the settlers' removal of the trees caused the nutrients in the soil to leach away and be washed downhill, where they formed an impregnable layer of 'hard pan', which impeded drainage. The land above became acidic and toxic to everything but heathers and rushes, to the extent that by 2500 BC it had been abandoned, while the lower reaches were becoming waterlogged because of the impermeable hard pan. Since the ground was extremely wet and acidic, the natural process of soil rejuvenation couldn't happen, and so peat began to form instead, building up year upon year into an endless black heather-clad mantel hugging the topography like a homespun blanket. Hence the term 'blanket bog'.

Whether this was caused by human interference or climate change, the upshot was that by the end of the Bronze Age, about 500 BC, farmers had been forced to abandon the uplands and began clearing the denser forests in the valleys. The blanket bog continued to rise and spread, and by the arrival of the Normans in the twelfth century it covered vast swathes of Ireland's uplands and was encroaching on lower land. By the seventeenth century it had reached three metres deep in parts, and it was then that people began to cut it as turf for fuel.

In contrast, raised bogs developed far earlier and for different reasons. They began in the hollows left by glacial moraines that filled with water to form small lakes after the ice age nine thousand years ago. Over time, reeds grew around their edges and as they died and rotted they created peaty soil, which allowed them to extend further into the lake. Over many years the peat built up, choking the lake, until by about 1500 BC only small areas of open water remained. The increased rainfall and the sodden, sponge-like bogs caused the water table to rise, resulting in the area around it becoming increasingly wet and stagnant. Nothing but mosses could grow on it, and each year as the mosses decomposed they made the bog rise higher until it became a vast bulge covering the lowlands.

About 500 BC the climate turned drier for a spell, and trees were able to become established on the bogs. But once the rains returned, the trees rotted back into the peat, creating the great trunks of bog oak and bog pine we find there today. These raised bogs expanded just like the blanket bogs, extending their stagnant waters into surrounding woodlands and consuming them too. By the eighteenth century some bogs were up to 12 metres in depth, the mean depth being 7 metres. These were then harnessed by humans for fuel.

How do bogs remember so much? Principally, it is because they create an oxygen-deficient environment that is the result of their saturation. The microbes and fungi that would normally decay organic material cannot develop and a vast array of microscopic pollen grains and single-celled organisms survive, as well as seeds, insects and myriad other things. Together these provide a remarkably accurate picture of elements, such as the species that proliferated, the wetness of the climate and the nutrient status of the ground.

The bogs show evidence of new algal productivity in lake beds from eleven thousand years ago, which means that the weather must have warmed up, and we can extrapolate that this must have coincided with the retreat of the ice sheet and the restoration of the warm Atlantic currents around Ireland. Reading the pollen chart of a bog shows us evidence of the first hardy species of grasses to arrive on the newly bare, postglacial land. In higher strata we find the pollen of the crowberries that followed them and then the rugged little juniper bushes that would have crawled across the harsh tundra, growing bigger and bushier with every warming year, inadvertently preparing the soil for its competitor, the birch tree. All this is evident from simply pushing a metal tube into the bog to extract a core sample of its sediment layers and then examining the distinctive pores and patterns of the pollen spores in each layer under a microscope.

Armed with a clear pollen report for an area, we can retrace in our mind the evolutionary steps taken to reach the present landscape. We can picture the first stoic pioneer birch tree that would have arrived in the area and that sent out 15 million feather-light seeds, year after year, to take over the land from the juniper and crowberry and unwittingly enrich it for others.

The pollen record will probably reveal the presence of some pine trees scattered through the region too, and by about ten thousand years ago there is evidence in the record of the arrival of the hazel tree. From my own few acres in Co. Westmeath, I see how hazel will sprout even in shade, so it's no surprise that soon hazel managed to outcompete the birch by growing up from under it and crowding it out. But what is surprising is just how extensively it spread. The pollen records show that the microscopic sperm-carrying reproductive bodies of hazel catkins were seventeen times more abundant than all other tree species put together.

Forest must have stretched in every direction ten thousand years ago. The core samples demonstrate that there was only a tiny proportion of non-tree pollen in the landscape. It's hard to picture the island almost completely covered in hazel wood, as nothing like it survives today, apart from the stunted hazel thickets of the Burren, which are low and dense from growing in denuded soils on limestone rock. Predictably, the records show that the hazel too was eventually outcompeted by taller, mightier species, such as the oak and the elm, which grew above the hazel, confining it to the status of an under-shrub, where it produced little pollen to be logged in the bog archives.

If we continue scanning the stratified layers of the pollen record, we can see that by about eight thousand years ago alder had arrived and was spreading rapidly. This presumably meant that the climate had become wetter, as alder thrives on wet ground, which is a good example of how bogs record just as much about climate as they do about plant species. For example, an experienced palaeoclimatologist can spot fine sand layers in a core sample from coastal bogs that are evidence of particularly intense Atlantic storms in which sand from beaches or dunes is whipped up and carried inland. Layers with high sand content reflect decades or even centuries of intense and frequent storms. We can even date some of these events, as the bog will preserve the dust-like glassy shards from ash blasted into the air by volcanic eruptions in Iceland. And by matching these 'tephra' layers to known eruption dates of specific volcanoes, we can accurately date a particular layer of the bog.

Accumulating peat seals and protects everything it covers, from microscopic remnants that provide contextual evidence of environmental processes to macroscopic remains in the form of archaeological sites, artefacts and larger plant and animal remains. And though the pollen won't record much about the animals that were enticed to these woodlands, other palaeo-environmental records do show evidence of the giant deer, the reindeer, the hare, the otter, the Irish stoat, the badger and the natterjack toad, as well as other birds, bats and insects that populated the land. And plants too, of course, such as St Dabeoc's heath, fleabane, kidney saxifrage and the arbutus tree.

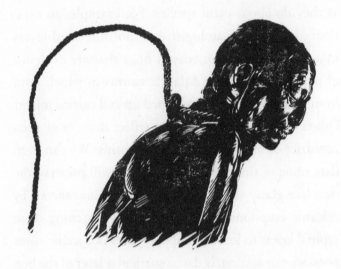

BOG BODIES

By far the most significant and poignant marker for humans in any pollen record from a raised bog is the increase in grasses and plants of disturbed ground from about six thousand years ago, when Neolithic settlers first arrived with their cattle and crop plants. This marks the beginning of it all: human settlement on the island, when farmers started cutting down forests to make room for their cattle and corn, setting in motion the loss of fertility of much of western Ireland. It's all there, recorded in the reproductive bodies of plants that drifted on the wind and came to rest on a bog, where they were faithfully preserved.

In fact, we find within the bog's memory banks perfectly preserved examples of the equipment that farmers used to shape the land and set in train the process of its degradation. The tools of stone, copper, bronze and iron – evolving in that order – are found lying at levels that can be correlated with the vegetation history by analysing the pollen that clings to them. In a single bog you may find a stone axe head of the first farmers who cut into the postglacial forest, right up to an Iron Age ploughshare, and, near the surface, a titanium bolt from a mechanical turf harvester, all tools for exploiting natural resources and shaping the landscape.

Even more poignant, though, is to come upon human remains, not just ghostly memories of their past actions or the detritus of their practices, or the gaseous emissions from which their old fables arose. The vinegar-like waters of high bogs are so acidic that a body that ends up engulfed in one is more likely to be pickled than to decompose. The sphagnum moss binds both nitrogen and oxygen, further inhibiting bacterial growth, and the oak trunks, boughs and roots that are entombed within most bogs release their tannins into the water, which then tan human skin, just like tanning cowhide. The natural humic acid in the sour water also helps.

If you've ever tried pickling cucumbers, you know the importance of adding tannin-rich grape leaves, tea leaves or oak leaves to prevent them from turning to mush. The bog wood does the same for humans. The only part that degrades is the bones, which can be leached of calcium and gradually demineralise. But the rest of the body – flesh, internal organs, hair, nails and clothing – can survive for millennia.

More than a hundred bodies have been found in Irish bogs, and while some appear to have become mired in it and drowned, others were buried formally, and others again seem to have been disposed of hurriedly and secretively. The most startling examples are the truly ancient bodies that suddenly emerge out of the bog while people are cutting turf. These unfortunate figures appear to have been victims of torture rituals and were then buried as part of a gruesome ceremony.

The oldest of these is known as Cashel Man, who dates from over four thousand years ago. He was discovered near Port Laoise in 2011 and is said to be the oldest European bog body yet found with skin intact. There are also Old Croghan Man from Co. Offaly, Clonycavan Man from Co. Meath, Gallagh Man from Co. Galway, Baronstown West Man from Co. Kildare, Derryvarroge Man from Co. Kildare, Kinakinelly Man from Co. Galway, Ballgudden Woman (now lost) from somewhere in Ulster, Drumkeeragh Body (probably female) from Co. Down and Ballygroll Child (also lost) from somewhere in Ulster. Some are skeletons, but most have just skin, flesh and hair.

The majority are male, possibly because men are more likely to inflict violence on each other and be in positions of wealth or power that would attract the ritualistic violence of others. Many also suffered horrendous acts of cruelty, such as having their nipples ripped off and their skull smashed in. I thought at first that going to see these desiccated victims in a museum would be off-putting or gory, but in fact the bodies inspire a strange feeling of tenderness and awe. The terror that accompanied their death has been leached away with their bones, and what remains is a visceral sense of their residual strength, their gaunt beauty and imposing character.

Whenever I'm in Dublin with time on my hands, I sidle into the National Museum in Kildare Street to spend time with these forebears of ours that the land has contrived to preserve and carry into our world. The first one I got to know was Clonycavan Man, who was found in 2003 in Clonycavan bog, near Ballivor in Co. Meath. He is an imposing figure with a thin beard, dyed red by the bog's tannins, and a hairline that is shaved high to extend his forehead and guide your attention upwards to his remarkable hairstyle, in which the strands fold forwards and then back on top of themselves to give a Mohawk effect.

Clonycavan Man's beautifully tanned skin, toned like burnished leather, coaxes the eyes to linger. This is no skeleton of bleached bones but a fleshed-out individual whose pores are still visible. When we look at his bold, determined face, with its squashed nose and slightly crooked teeth, it feels as if he is still present in a palpable way despite having died about 300 BC.

He has already communicated much about his life to us, from the fact that he was eating mainly fresh fruit and vegetables in the months before he died to the intriguing finding that the gel he used to hold his dramatic hairstyle in place was made of vegetable oil and resin from a pine tree that does not grow in Ireland. The nearest location for the pine trees that produced the resin is northern Spain and southern France, along the Pyrenees. So, we know that 2,300 years ago this man was informed and affluent enough to obtain his haircare products from over one thousand kilometres away.

His re-emergence into our world was a violent one, in the teeth of an industrial peat-harvester that tore off his legs and hands; but when you're in the company of his remaining body (head, neck, arms, torso and upper abdomen) you don't get the feeling that he is in any way diminished. He is still a strong, compelling presence. In fact, when he was found in 2003 the local people felt that it was the body of a deceased neighbour rather than ancient remains, and they called in the Garda Technical Bureau instead of the National Museum. The crime forensic team found that he had been struck twice with a sharp implement, most likely an axe. One blow caused a large laceration across the bridge of his nose and under his right eye, and a second split his skull open, causing a deep wound in which parts of his brain were found.

This violent end is reminiscent of an even more evocative bog body unearthed, also in 2003, near Croghan Hill, Co. Offaly, and known as Old Croghan Man. He was stabbed in the chest, struck in the neck, decapitated and cut in half. Then hazel rods were threaded through holes in his upper arms, as though he were being spancelled or trussed like an animal. But again, when you see Old Croghan Man today, his suffering is not what strikes you; instead, it's the elegance of his bearing.

From the length of his torso and arms, osteo-archaeologists are confident that he was about 6 feet 6 inches tall. His fingers and hands are soft and free of scars, revealing that he had probably never engaged in manual labour. In fact, the only blemish is the equivalent of two small paper cuts on one hand. His nails are just as perfect and seem to have been manicured. Even his fingerprints are still clearly visible.

Just like Clonycavan Man, he was found naked, which marks the bodies out from most accidentally drowned or hastily buried bodies. These men appear to have been stripped and buried in the bog in the knowledge that they would never decompose – an act of humiliation, perhaps, or a sacrifice to the gods. Also, both men had their nipples sliced off before they died, or at least they suffered some form of wound that caused their nipples to perish.

This is of interest because accounts of kingship in regions along the Eurasian border and North Africa make specific reference to the practice of nipple-sucking as a means of pledging loyalty. St Patrick wrote in his Confessio in the fifth century that when he fled Ireland he was offered passage on a boat by some sailors, but he refused to suck their nipples.

St Patrick lived eight hundred years after these men, but sucking the nipple is believed to have been a practice that endured as a way of acknowledging a king's direct connection with the life force of the earth goddess, and it therefore became a way for subjects to display their deference. Some archaeologists argue that removing the men's nipples was a way of decommissioning them if they had failed to bring peace and plenty to their kingdom by collaborating in a fruitful way with the natural energies of the earth. Alternatively, these men may have been candidates for kingship who had failed to establish their leadership and were maimed and then ritually killed as a warning to others, or as a sacrifice to the gods.

Both Clonycavan Man and Old Croghan Man also appear to have been 'killed' three times: by strangulation, stabbing and drowning, lending credence to the idea that it was a ritualised killing of some type, possibly in recognition that the earth goddess had three core aspects, and the death ritual therefore needed to sever the king's connection with all three aspects.

It's not the violent death endured by Old Croghan Man that will affect you most: it's his humanity. An analysis of his nails tells us that his diet in the months before his death, between 362 and 175 BC, was rich in meat and other protein and that his final meal, as revealed by analyses of the contents in his stomach, consisted of a rough gruel of cereal and buttermilk – a peasant meal that may have been a humiliation for someone of his stature and discerning tastes.

We do not know the names of Old Croghan Man or Clonycavan Man, nor the languages they spoke, nor what they thought and what they believed; but we do know that their killers tried to obliterate them – and that they failed. I find myself speaking Irish to them when I visit them and being thrilled by the notion that, if they did wake up, they might be able to understand me.

I tell them how grateful I am that they managed to leap the time–space barrier and make it into our world. *D'éirigh leo an bás a shárú*: they triumphed over death. When I'm with them I close my eyes and imagine them standing before me with their families, or partner, by their side and a child in their arms, possibly with a beloved hound by their feet. All are dressed in their most elaborate regalia, in my mind's eye, as colourful and evocative as those worn by the Icelandic chieftains at Þingvellir.

Every time I see the wound on the arm of Old Croghan Man, it's as if I can see him raising up his elbow to protect himself from the blows being inflicted on him. But it's to no avail: eventually he can no longer fend off the weapon that stabs through his chest. There's a similar arm wound on one of the other figures, Cashel Man, who died almost 1,300 years earlier, and archaeologists believe it may also be the result of a defensive reaction as he was being put to death. When I see the hairs on his skin standing just as they did when he last breathed life in the Early Bronze Age, the hairs on my own skin rise in response.

These figures are embodiments of ourselves but from the far-distant past. A crucial lesson they have for us is just how rooted we have always been to the landscape. The former Keeper of Antiquities at the National Museum, Dr Ned Kelly, noticed that many of the sacrificed bodies were buried in border areas. Cashel Man was found at the edge of the territory of Fearann Ua Leathlobhair that is overlooked by Cros Dubh, or Crosy Duff Hill, the probable inauguration site of the regional kings of Laois. A selection of what appear to be votive offerings to the earth have been found in the same area, including bog butter and axe heads of stone and copper. These appear to have been deposited as ritual offerings to appease or show gratitude to the gods, or to act as energetic markers at the edge of their territory.

Old Croghan Man was buried on the boundary of another important midland territory, Tuath Cruachan, but 1,300 years later. His burial site was also overlooked by the inauguration site of the kings of that region, Croghan Hill. If both men were indeed buried beneath the inauguration hills where they had once been crowned as kings on the borders of their kingdoms, it is further evidence that the ritual of kingship survived in Ireland for thousands of years, from at least as far back as the Early Bronze Age, and continued to some degree right up to the end of the Middle Ages, when the Gaelic way of life was finally destroyed.

A YEAR'S FIRE

I've said that bogs have been industrialised and destroyed by Bord na Móna, but I've also pointed out that 16 per cent of the country is still clad in bogs. It's hard to imagine both statements being true. In reality, there are many different types of bog. *Easca* is a sedgy bog or mountainside; *mulchán* is a wet mud-filled bog; *corrach* is low-lying soggy bog; *ride* is a bog mire; and *móinín* is a little marshy bog. The likelihood is that any bog you encounter will have had much of its turf already extracted in the past few hundred years.

What you see in such places is the empty space that once had the accumulated remains of thousands of years of every pollen grain, hazel branch, yew root, eel bone, oak trunk, wolf skin and human body that was partially decomposed into it. You'll notice that the edge lines where humans stopped cutting are marked by a series of shaggy banks sliced into the landscape. In some places the absent peat will once have extended up to ten metres above your head. It's hard to imagine in parts of the midlands that you are standing far below where ground level was a century ago.

What we see today are the final seams from which a particular family or individual or industrial enterprise had been cutting turf for years, decades or even lifetimes – depending on the depth and quality of the turf. These seams are called *oitreacha móna, cois mhóna* or *bachtaí*, and they are made up of the *eanach*, which is the uncut part, and the *fáslach* or *gabhal portaigh* or *lagphortach*, which is the bit that has been cut away – the vacuum, the emptiness, of which only the ground level remains. This represents the point where the peat 'bottomed out' – where the turf-cutters reached the impermeable layer of puddled clay or panned mineral-clogged soil on which the bog had first begun to grow thousands of years before. This is where you'll find scorch marks from fires set by Neolithic farmers to burn down the trees that were originally here. This is also where the newly cut turf is laid out to dry.

Other features you might see are *sconsaí*, which are ditches made by cutting away a line of turf, and *criathrach*, which are the perilous bog holes that inspired our fear of bogs. It was a *sconsa* rather than a *criathrach* that swallowed Kerri ní Dochartaigh, but you'd normally be able to see a *sconsa*, while a *criathrach* will tend to be covered in moss and grass and thus be invisible.

In northern parts of Ireland there'll often be three large steps cut into the bank at its furthest edge. They are there to make bogs a little safer, or at least to protect against a curse that St Colm Cille puts on those greedy enough to extract all the turf and leave nothing behind. It is said that the saint was once trapped in a bog and couldn't flee to safety because of the steep banks. He therefore placed this curse so that the same predicament wouldn't befall others. The story serves as a reminder to leave the bog traversable for those who might pass through it, but it's also part of the practice that is common in sustainable communities all over the world to leave a share of any natural element for the land itself, or for the fairies, or simply for good luck.

When we stand on the edge of a bank looking out over the ghostly remnant of what had once been a forest or a lake – and then a dense, multilayered mass of decomposed organic matter that had been cut, dried and burnt for cooking and heating – it's not hard to summon up the people who shaped the landscape.

It was the slanesman who first dug out a bank and cut into the open seam to extract individual sods of turf, which were then flicked to a barrowman, who stacked them on an open-sided bog barrow. When the barrow was fully laden, it was wheeled to the 'spread' site – the bottomed-out bog. The neatness of the slanesman's work was of central importance. Keeping a 'straight face' – a sheer, vertical façade – was vital. A messy slanesman was known as a 'clod cutter'.

There were two principal ways in which he could carve the sods: from the high bank above or from the low bank below, facing straight into the seam. A *sleán*, or slane, was his sculpting tool – a down slane for cutting from above and a breast slane from below. Both are a form of turf spade with an L-shaped or square-bladed piece of metal attached to a long handle. There were variations throughout the country, adapted to local conditions and techniques and the preferences of the slanesman. A crucial difference was the shape and thickness of the *binn sleáin*, which is its flange or side wing. Occasionally, a *cairbreán* was used instead, which is more narrow-bladed, or a *baisín*, which has a square head, or a *deibín*, which has a triangular head, like a paint-scraper.

While the pressure was on the slanesman, he was only as good as his accomplices, the catcher and the barrowman. He would send the sods flying through the air, and it was up to the catcher to grab them and stack them right over the centre line of the barrow, running from front to back, with both the top and bottom tier being laid on the flat at right angles to this line and halved on it, so that it would then be possible for the barrowman to tip them out correctly on the spread site.

The practice of hurling sods in a discourteously fast and careless manner was known as *radadh*, which can also refer to flinging anything in a hasty way. These sods were large and heavy and could be made up of as much as 95 per cent water. A dry sod is a *caorán*, while these wet ones were referred to as *spairteanna, torpáin, sliobáin* or *spaid*. A clumsy catcher of a *dóid mhór mhóna* ('big sod of turf') was known as being *spadach* ('clod-footed').

Just as every slanesman had his favourite catcher, who could work in graceful synchronicity with him, a catcher relied on a skilled barrowman who, once the barrow was loaded with between a dozen and a score of sods, would wheel it over the uneven surface of heather and bog grass tussocks to the spreading-ground without disturbing the catcher's careful placement. The barrowman would then tip the barrow to one side in just the right way to allow the sods to slide off and stand on their ends on the ground in a line. It required both skill and luck to drop the sods, one double row at a time, standing end up and in rows, without breaking a sod. Too many broken sods were a blot of shame that would be remarked on by others.

In small families the roles of catcher and barrowman were taken by the one person, whereas if the distance between the turf bank and spread site was great, more than one barrowman would be needed. The ideal situation was to have two slanesmen and their support teams working a bank at the same time. This was how to live up to the proverb *Lá mona tine bhliana* ('A day's work on the bog is a year's fire').

A good slanesman could cut a *sleán* of turf in a day, which is a quarter and a half of turf, or twelve loads. A quarter of turf is twenty feet long, eight feet wide and three feet high. There are thirty *cis* in a quarter, a *cis* being the amount of turf required to fill a large basket. A typical horse load would consist of five *cis*, but a large horse load could have six of them. A *cis* is different from a *críol* of turf, which was a smaller donkey's load. There were therefore six horse loads in a quarter, so a single man could cut one-and-a-quarter big cartloads of turf in a day. Two teams working the same bank should manage two-and-a-half big cartloads, which might just do a small household through the winter.

The words for big turf loads were matched with other words for the smaller loads used at home, such as the *scib* or *sciath* of turf that children would bring in from the barn each morning. This is the amount that fits into a willow basket, called a *sciath*. It could be topped up during the day with a *gabháil* or two, which is the amount of dried turf you can hold between your arms and your chest.

But there were many more steps between cutting the turf and bringing it home. It needed to be left on the spread for a few days or weeks to firm up; the women and children would then join the men to help turn the sods again to ensure consistent drying. They were then left another few weeks before *cruiceadh* (or *cnuchairt* or *gróigeadh*) *na móna* ('footing the turf'), which involved stacking five to twelve sods in either a Jenga or wigwam shape so that air could pass through them. These were called *coirceoga*, *gróigeáin* or *cnuchairí* ('footings' or 'gogeens'). After a few more weeks they were restacked into *dúchán* or *somadáin* (small clamps) or occasionally into large ones, *púcóga* or *caisil*, so that they could dry further. Finally, in August or September they were brought home by cart and built into *cruacha*, big ricks that are like clamps but larger, and this then became the winter fuel supply.

Of course, no two clamps were alike because they were all dependent on the type of peat that was in the bank. There were seven or eight 'spits' in a typical midland bank, a spit being a layer of about the depth of a *sleán* (roughly 22cm). Generally, the first and second spits were considered white turf or sponge turf. It's light and easily broken and only really useful for starting a fire, as it ignites readily but gives off little heat. It was generally left on the high bank to dry. Then comes brown turf, of medium density. It is not easily broken and gives off moderate heat when burnt. Most of the bank consists of spits of brown turf.

And then right at the bottom, if you're lucky, you'll find a spit or two of stone turf or black turf, which is the densest and the longest-burning of the three. It will bake a loaf of bread or boil a pot of stew, and it leaves behind a distinctive brown ash. Cutting stone turf is called 'bottoming', which must be done quickly, as the groundwater can start bursting up from beneath. Neighbours will tend to help when bottoming a bank to get the most extracted before it floods.

Of course, many areas in Ireland had no bogs, or perhaps had less mature ones that might be only a thousand years old rather than many thousands of years. These tended to be wetter and less compacted, and the only way to extract fuel from them was by making something called 'mud turf', whereby you dug out the soft, wet, black mud and broke it up with graips or strong forks. This was then wetted to form a pancake-like batter, and you waded into it barefoot and started scooping out handfuls and forming them into sods as you would a snowball. This practice is called 'baking' and could produce high-quality fuel, but it was messy. You needed plenty of water nearby to frequently clean your hands and smooth down the sod, as you would with plaster. In a good summer the sods would dry out, shrinking to a small fraction of their original size. They could then be footed, clamped and ricked like ordinary turf.

The crucial part of this is 'in a good summer', for in those wet years, the likes of which helped create the bogs in the first place, the sods wouldn't dry and the results could be catastrophic. There was no alternative fuel for heating or cooking. People stripped the landscape of any remaining bushes or twigs and then would burn furniture, fish bones, cow dung – anything that might produce enough heat to boil potatoes and cook porridge and keep people warm through the coldest nights.

Industrial turf-cutting has ended and cutting for domestic use is coming to a natural end as a new generation have access to easier supplies of fuel and are no longer willing to exert the effort required. But the grip of peatland on our imagination is still strong. Not only was it connected with an eerie darkness, but it was also known as a place of excitement and playfulness during those few sunny days when the whole community, from the very young to the elderly, would gather on the bog to foot and stack turf.

There was a festiveness to those long summer days that offered an escape from the farmyard routine and a chance to live *al fresco*, boiling eggs and tea on bog fires in the company of friends and neighbours. The novelty brought with it a loosening of inhibitions and a relaxation of social conventions that enabled everyone, young couples especially, to interact in a carefree, instinctive way – to be more playful, more flirtatious, free from the eyes of the clergy, who controlled so much of social engagement. This was as much a tonic as the bitter juice made from the long stalks of bog bean that grew in the watery mire and that was taken to cleanse the blood and replenish vitality in springtime, or as the frogspawn collected from these same mires and pools and fermented for a year in darkness for use as an anti-inflammatory.

Nowadays, all the attention is on the environmental role of peatland since the realisation that it can accumulate carbon from the air at a rate of up to 0.7 tonnes per hectare per year, sequestering it and then storing it for thousands of years if left undisturbed and if the water table is not artificially lowered. What we once dismissed as the most useless part of our landscape turns out to be the most viable long-term carbon store in the terrestrial biosphere. Every cut that we continue to make into the bog, and every drain we dig, compromises this, sending not only buried carbon into the atmosphere but methane too, which is twenty-three times more polluting to the upper atmosphere.

The abandoned, post-industrial bogs that have been stripped of their turf aren't capturing carbon. In fact, they're emitting it, but reflooding them can stop the emissions and begin the process of reviving the bogs to a state in which they can begin capturing carbon again. This is what is planned for much of the midlands so that habitats can be restored for the many rare and endangered bog birds such as the *cearc fhraoigh* (red grouse, literally 'hen of the heather'), *fuiseog mhóna* (meadow pipit, literally 'bog lark') and carnivorous plants such as *drúchtín móna* (sundew, literally 'little dew of the bog').

Peatland will probably also continue its role as a source of inspiration to artists and writers. The great post-war avant-garde artist Joseph Beuys described these spongy realms as the 'liveliest elements in the European landscape, not just from the point of view of flora, fauna, birds and animals, but as storing places of life, mystery and chemical change, preservers of ancient history'. And certainly, from a cultural point of view, peatlands have been a prime inspiration for centuries, since at least the nineteenth century, when a fashion for bog oak sculpture took hold in Dublin and Killarney, leading to the production of endless brooches, bracelets, walking sticks and furniture. Then, in the years after independence, peatland became a popular scene in Irish art, with bucolic vistas of blanket bog cloaking statuesque hills in paintings by Paul Henry and Maurice MacGonigal.

The arrival of Beuys in Ireland in 1974, and his creation of *Irish Energy*, a sculpture consisting of a thick layer of Kerrygold butter sandwiched between two peat briquettes, brought bogs to the attention of the international art world. At about that time, the English-born artist Barrie Cooke began painting vast canvases featuring the great 'Irish elk', which were displayed prominently in public buildings and at major exhibitions throughout the 1980s. These paintings captured the grandeur of both the Irish elk (later proved to be a form of deer) and the bog itself. They consisted of skeletal forms on a peat background of treacly tones of ruby and mustard. It was as if the deer bones were being animated by the vibrancy of the bog, siphoning a marrow transfusion from it. These brought home to many people the epic drama of our peatland expanses, as did Cooke's great friend Seamus Heaney, who was equally bog-enchanted at the time. His 'bog poems' of the 1970s offered a new prism through which to see them, both in their own right, in poems like 'Bogland',

> We have no prairies
> To slice a big sun at evening
> [...] Our unfenced country
> Is bog that keeps crusting
> Between the sights of the sun.

and as multi-tangential metaphors for social and ethical issues, in particular the political turmoil in the North, addressed in poems about the bog men, such as 'The Tollund Man' and 'Strange Fruit', with its eerie description:

Here is the girl's head like an exhumed gourd.
Oval-faced, prune-skinned, prune-stones for
teeth.

After Beuys, turf became totemic in contemporary
art, appearing in milled and solid form in works of art
such as Carl Andre's turf sod installation at Rosc '84. But
it wasn't until 2000 that the Bord na Móna briquette
regained international attention in art, when the architect
Tom de Paor used 21 tonnes of them to build Ireland's
first pavilion at the Venice Biennale. His installation,
titled *N3*, was corbelled, like an early Christian oratory
or Neolithic passage tomb, on the edge of Venice. Once
the Biennale was over, the 40,000-odd rectangles of
midland bog were mulched and spread in the Giardini
as a gift of ground to a drowning city.

Perhaps the high-water mark in the history of peatland art was reached in 2002 with the establishment
of Sculpture in the Parklands, on twenty hectares of
cut-away bog at Lough Boora Discovery Park, Co. Offaly.
It's one of the most remarkable landscapes in Ireland,
consisting of a barren expanse of flat, linear planes that
stretch to the horizon in every direction like some lunar
nightmare or a brown desert salt flat. Inserted into this
post-industrial dead zone are over twenty vast sculptural
installations of glacial stone, iron girders, bog wood
and decommissioned industrial extraction equipment

that rise up into the broad midland skies. After years of exposure to the harsh climate, the materials are now wonderfully weathered, and they are harmonising with, and still lording over, the empty landscape.

As if this juxtaposition of contemporary art and a spent wasteland created out of the compacted remains of thousands of years of decomposed rushes and mosses weren't heady enough, right in the heart of the park an astounding discovery was made. Remnants were found of a hunter-gatherer campsite that is almost as old as the settlement at Mount Sandel in Coleraine. Charcoal patches that appear to be the remains of hearths from 8,500 or 9,000 years ago were uncovered beneath the peat from a time before the bogs ever had a chance to form. Alongside them were more than 1,500 artefacts from that time, including stone axe heads, spear points, blades made of a flint-like material and the burnt bones of wild pig, wild-fowl and fish that would have been eaten about 6800 BC.

Standing at the site of a storm beach that was once on the edge of a massive postglacial lake originally connected to the Shannon, where Ireland's early nomadic Mesolithic settlers would have hunted and cooked their food, makes abundantly clear the ability of land to preserve memory better than anything else. That is, if we have the skill to read it properly.

When I'm at Lough Boora I like to think of the lake that these forebears had visited becoming gradually so clogged up with its own debris and the mass of moss peat that gathered over millennia that it rose higher and higher, until eventually a solid sponge of fibrous bog ten metres tall was formed, stretching over 25,000 acres. And then this was gradually cut away over seventy short years and transported on a specially constructed narrow-gauge railway line, leaving a vacuum behind it.

But as we know, nature abhors a vacuum, and wild-life soon returned to the emptiness. Lough Boora is now a refuge for more than 130 species of birds, including spectacular numbers of whooper swans, golden plovers, lapwings and the last remaining population of native grey partridge in Ireland.

CROGHAN HILL

We can't really leave bogs behind without at least touching on the vast prairie-like plains of the Bog of Allen, which covers almost one thousand square kilometres between the River Shannon and the River Liffey and is the source of the River Boyne. It stretches across parts of Cos. Offaly, Meath, Laois and Westmeath but is primarily associated with Co. Kildare, where it was described in the seventeenth century as the 'Notorious Red Bog of Ely' by the surveyor and cartographer Sir William Petty.

There's even a tale of the pagan goddess Brigid getting into difficulty on the bog on her way to surrender to the authority of the Christian faith and take vows from the Bishop of Croghan, who resided on a significant landmark called Croghan Hill, which rises like a green oasis in its centre. One of the bishop's pupils, Mac Caille, came upon her wandering in a lost and distraught manner and warned, 'The way is trackless, with marshes, deserts, bogs and pools.' This hill rising from a flat expanse is reminiscent of the assembly sites we've already encountered; certainly, Croghan Hill too was a known gathering point for millennia and was the inauguration site of the kings of that region.

Any site like this at a higher elevation in the landscape was probably used for assemblies, fairs, markets or gatherings at some point, and certainly that was the case with Croghan Hill. In fact, we encountered it before when dealing with Old Croghan Man, who was found near its base. As an extinct volcano 230 metres high, it was ideal because it was elevated but not high enough to require a steep climb, and it was visible from most parts of northern Co. Offaly. It was reasonably accessible, although knowledge of the route would have been required, as Brigid discovered to her cost. Stretches of it were perilous to the uninitiated right into the nineteenth and twentieth centuries, when large-scale land drainage initiatives were carried out. A guide would have been needed to steer visitors safely across.

There's a fascinating reference to the hill in a mythical tale known as 'The Boyhood Deeds of Fionn', which recounts how the men of Ireland would travel to Croghan Hill at Samhain to woo a beautiful maiden whose palace was inside the hill. Each year someone would be killed in some gruesome way in the course of this wooing. It's intriguing to speculate on Old Croghan Man's harsh ending in light of this.

The woman they were after was known as Éile, who was an elusive, Otherworldly deity who was sister to the fairy queen Méabh of Connacht and resided inside the hill. It was thought that her body and her chariot are buried beneath one of the mounds that are visible in and around a Bronze Age fort that crowns the hilltop. The four external embankments and ditches of this fort, as on the Hill of Ward, make it clear that this was a significant assembly area even three or four thousand years ago. The old name for the hill is Cruachán Brí Éile, with *cruachán* meaning a prominent round-topped hill and Brí possibly referring to the pagan goddess, and later Christian saint, Brigid.

Local folklore says that the hill opens at Samhain, offering access to the Otherworld, and that this is why the men came in search of the woman in the palace. The story goes that the men of Ireland were at feud with her and that, one after another, they would seek her out in the hope that she would surrender to them, but on every occasion either they or one of their retinue would be killed.

If this story of the men of Ireland wooing Éile at Samhain sounds familiar, it's because it's a version of the story of the male seeking to gain dominance over the female forces animating the land and culture that we've come upon so often in these pages. It's at the kernel of the tale of the maiden Brigid coming to Croghan Hill to submit to the bishop, and of Conaire Mór sending his druid harpist to capture Princess Tuag, and of the young man who tried to steal Áine's green cloak at Lough Gur.

In the seventh century, Bishop Tírechán recorded another incidence of this in the story of how St Patrick gathered at a place called Cruachu (which is either Croghan Hill or Rathcroghan, Co. Roscommon) with an assembly of bishops. There he encountered two powerful female figures from the area, the fair-haired Eithne and the red-haired Feidheilm, who had come to wash themselves at a well on the hill.

The women were startled by the unusual appearance of these bearded, tonsured men, who presumably were dressed in elaborate robes and may have been carrying shiny, bejewelled mitres. They enquired politely about who these strangers were who had turned up at their morning washing spot, and Patrick replied, with the testiness common to many petulant preachers, 'It would be better for you to profess our true God than to ask questions about our race.'

The women, according to Bishop Tírechán's account, had no idea what he was referring to and asked him:

> Who is God and where is God and whose God is he and where is his dwelling-place? Has your God sons and daughters, gold and silver? Is he in the sky or in the earth or in the water, in rivers, in mountains, in valleys?

Patrick moulded his reply to suit these unabashed pagan women:

> Our God is the God of heaven and earth, of the sea and the rivers, God of the sun and the moon and all the stars, the God of high mountains and low valleys ... He breathes in all things, makes all things live, surpasses all things, supports all things; he illumines the light of the sun, he consolidates the light of the night and the stars ...

According to Tírechán, the women were enthralled by his words and pledged to surrender themselves to this new Christian god, although many other accounts insist that neither they nor their father, Lóegaire, who is described as 'a great king, fierce and pagan, emperor of the barbarians', ever agreed to succumb to Patrick.

The importance of the site long before St Patrick and his missionaries tried to take control of it, or even before Old Croghan Man was sacrificed here, is attested to by the Bronze Age fort on the summit and also by the fact that the hill was claimed in some accounts to have been the supernatural birthplace of the semi-divine River Shannon.

The goddess whose home this was, Éile, although elusive, was a powerful figure with ties to all sorts of other mythologies and core beliefs. The similarity of her name to that of the surrounding bog, the Bog of Allen, is noteworthy, or her name may derive from the word *álainn* ('beautiful'). This would link us back to the goddess Áine once again.

Indeed, there's an important mythical site named Cluain Áine that is said to be near Croghan Hill. Áine, you'll recall, means 'bright', 'brilliance' and 'delight', which seems to suggest that all these sites were places where the radiance of the divine female energy is celebrated and enshrined. This is what Christian missionaries were trying to usurp, and they succeeded to a large degree – but not entirely. People kept coming to Croghan Hill for assemblies and gatherings that were not only connected with the church or the graveyard that was later established on the site, just as they came to Teltown for reasons other than worshipping at the four churches.

In fact, Croghan Hill became an important location in the Late Middle Ages for the ruling tribe of the region, Uí Failghe, who based themselves here and appear to have used it as their inauguration site (just as Old Croghan Man's tribe had done in the Iron Age). It is the Uí Failghe tribe who gave their name to the county, Uíbh Fhailí, or Offaly.

The medieval annals refer to a Battle of Tóchar Cruachán Brí Eile, which took place in 1385 between the English and the men of Uí Failghe. The tribe easily defeated the English, and the fact that the word *tóchar* was in the name suggests that a trackway across the bog may have been the cause of the battle, or perhaps it was a reason for the victory by the Irish side. *Tóchar* refers to a routeway across a bog, and we've seen that the Bog of Allen was treacherous for those who didn't know the right path across its miry expanses. The fact that people went to war over a bog road makes it clear how important such roads once were in Ireland.

Nowadays, everywhere is drained and easily accessible, which makes the former geography of such sites harder to discern; but in the coming decades it's likely that we'll have to re-wet these bogs to mitigate increased flooding and to help capture carbon from the atmosphere. Soon we might have to once again hire a guide to show us the way across the bog, or even rent a kayak or a traditional willow-made coracle to access the hill from certain directions.

IGNORING THE
FAMINE

We need to make a significant course change now, as there is no way to discuss landscape in Ireland without addressing the Great Famine. It has had an effect on the countryside that is arguably as dramatic as the introduction of metallurgy and farming by Bronze Age settlers 4,500 years ago and as the development of blanket bogs along the west coast five hundred years later. To put it simply, Ireland was a very different country before and after the Famine years of the 1840s.

Although in the most basic terms the Famine was

caused by the failure of the potato crop from 1845 to 1851, one must look back to the preceding century and to how the population had been rising, from 3 million in 1730 to 4 million in 1781, largely as a result of the widespread availability and ease of cultivation of a tuber imported from South America in the sixteenth century.

By 1800 the population had risen to 5.6 million, and that continued to increase to a peak of 8.5 million in 1845. A large percentage of the people were concentrated in the most rocky, infertile parts of Munster and Connacht, which were the most inhospitable parts of Ireland. Eking out an existence there required resilience and ingenuity, but even a surfeit of these traits didn't ensure success. Luck came into it too.

Practically every unused arable patch in the region was used to grow the staple food crop, potato, which, when combined with milk products like cheese and buttermilk, provided a nutritious diet. Not only did cultivation extend into the most remote land, but so too did human occupation. The increased population required more houses than had ever been needed before or possibly since, although the stone huts and one-roomed windowless mud cabins would hardly be classed as houses today.

When blight struck the potato crop in 1845, it caused upheaval because so many people were dependent on it for their survival. And when the blight returned the following year, the consequences were catastrophic for the poorest and weakest, who had no reserves to fall back on. The year 1847 saw a relief from the disease, but by then the people had eaten or sold off whatever seed potato they had managed to keep, so it was of little benefit. In the following years it returned, on and off, compounding the already dire situation and leading to widespread starvation.

Most deaths during the Famine weren't from hunger but from what was commonly known as 'famine fever', a range of infectious diseases such as typhus, cholera, relapsing fever, tuberculosis and smallpox that proliferated in the weakened population, helped by the crowding together of hungry people and the neglect of personal and domestic hygiene.

The Famine is said to have lasted from 1845 to 1851, but there was severe crop failure and hunger in many of the years before and after. In 1847 a quarter of a million people emigrated, and three million were fed from soup kitchens. That summer the blight didn't strike, but by then the poorest were no longer in a position to tend their land, as they had been forced to commit themselves to public work schemes, building roads and walls in return for meagre government food rations.

Yet lack of food in the country was never really the central issue with the Famine. Ireland exported vast amounts of grain, butter, bacon, ham, livestock, peas, beans, salmon, herring and oysters throughout those years. The issue was that landlords and the merchant class chose to sell them for higher prices in Britain rather than distribute them at home. The Irish name An Gorta Mór ('The Great Hunger') is a more apt name, as the word 'famine' implies an extreme shortage of food, which there never was. If anything, the situation was closer to genocide: an elite class chose to withhold food from the poorest, who they regarded as an encumbrance to progress.

Maybe the term 'genoslaughter', coined by Brendan O'Leary, professor of political science at the University of Pennsylvania, is more accurate still, as it captures the callousness of the British government rather than its committed intention to wipe out the Irish race. A belief in divine providence and a commitment to *laissez-faire* politics was a key factor in Britain choosing not to intervene in Ireland's plight. This was compounded by a disdain for landlords in Ireland who Britain regarded as corrupt and inept. They were reluctant to offer any form of relief that might strengthen their position.

Whether it was genocide or genoslaughter, in total more than three million live animals were exported from Ireland between 1846 and 1850, more than the number of people who emigrated during the Famine years. Even the worst year, known as Black '47, saw an increase of a third in calf exports from Ireland. Huge amounts of grain were also exported, although a poor grain harvest in 1846 resulted in higher imports than exports for the following two years.

And so what effect did all this have on the landscape? The population of Connacht fell by nearly a third and that of Munster by a fifth. The two million people who died or emigrated left behind them empty fields, homes and barns. Whole villages were wiped out in the western counties, as were many scattered settlements and cultivated fields in more remote areas. Most of the less fertile upland fields have been idle ever since. Cities such as Dublin, Belfast and Cork grew as thousands rushed to escape hunger and build new lives for themselves away from the soil that they no longer had trust in. It caused a generation to lose their confidence in the land, alienating them from what had been a life-giving force and the basis of their existence.

The effect was so profound that still today, 180 years later, we as a nation don't seem ready to address the legacy of what our ancestors endured. The trauma is still too great to face head on. There is increasing evidence from psychotherapists and epigeneticists that experiences such as these have long-lasting physical and psychological effects on societies, and these must be addressed communally. For many of us, our grandparents' grandparents were alive at the time. It is not all that long ago, but we make little effort to remember it in public conversation or in the form of memorials in the landscape. We've tried to put it behind us and move on, which was heroic in some ways, but it has inevitably left scars and the legacy of unresolved trauma.

A century after the Famine no public commemoration was held. The nation was considered still too frail and uncertain of itself in the 1940s to cope with the sense of loss and tragedy. Likewise, at the 150th anniversary in the 1990s the state kept the commemorations muted, apart from commissioning a national memorial sculpture by the artist John Behan at the foot of Croagh Patrick, Co. Mayo. His work consists of a large bronze ship with skeletal figures strung from the rigging. It's an evocative piece, certainly, but its focus is on the ship, which is a symbol of hope and escape rather than on the despair, entrapment and death that was the reality for most of those who perished.

Such a symbol doesn't fully represent the reality for those who endured a slow, painful death after years of starvation. Even now as you drive around the country, you'll see countless memorials to minor incidents in the War of Independence and the Civil War but virtually no monuments to the Famine. The few that do exist avoid focusing on the appalling reality and instead shift focus to some more hopeful aspect of it, such as the presence of a soup kitchen. (This is in marked contrast with the many Famine monuments in North American cities, including Ireland Park in Toronto, which features sculptures of emaciated Famine victims by Rowan Gillespie that correspond to his sculptures of emigrants on Custom House Quay in Dublin.) The motivation may be to spare people's anxieties, or because we haven't yet contemplated what it means to lose a quarter of our population through starvation and fever. But by sparing ourselves we only compound the continued denial. We preserve the dysfunction that inevitably arises when dark things are left to fester and when wounds aren't allowed to heal.

Many of us feel a tinge of guilt about how our ancestors managed to survive when others starved. My paternal great-grandfather Michael Magan was born into a modestly affluent farm in Killashee, Co. Longford, in 1827. The family reared cattle and sheep, grew vegetables and cereals and kept some hens and pigs, and they would have been able to export and import easily through Dublin via the Royal Canal. My sense is that the Famine didn't affect them in any meaningful way.

My maternal great-great-grandfather Michael Joseph Rahilly married in Ballylongford in 1837. There he ran a small shop that sold everything from ham to hammers. He died in 1849, possibly from famine fever, as the Famine was still devastating that part of Co. Kerry. His widow was left running the shop while also rearing five children, and she even managed to send her eldest son to boarding school and on to study medicine. Her second-eldest, Richard, took over the shop and fathered my great-grandmother Nell Humphreys (née Rahilly) and her brother Michael Joseph, later known as The O'Rahilly. The Famine certainly had more of an effect on them than on the Magans, but they bounced back quickly, and by the 1890s their shop and its ancillary business was worth £100,000 – about €15 million in today's terms.

Should I be proud of that, or feel some shame? Did both families do all they could to help their less affluent neighbours? I'll never know.

SCARS ON THE LANDSCAPE

Since neither the state nor our national consciousness have been able to come to terms with the full impact of the Famine, it's up to us to read the signs of it in the landscape ourselves. They are everywhere, if we choose to look. The most apparent are the linear ridges that run as corrugations up and down through the landscape. These undulations represent the trauma wrinkles of past experience. You'll see them not just on arable fields but right up to even the steepest summits and out on the remotest islands that you'd imagine would be cultivated only in desperation. These are remains of 'lazy beds', cultivation ridges that were used for growing mainly potatoes and corn. They were fashioned by spade or shovel, though some were carved out with a plough or mattock.

Sods were cut from the trenches on either side and inverted, hence the term 'lazy', as it was considered an easy way to make a ridge without having to dig up the central mound. Anyone who has tried it will realise that it is far from easy and that it actually adds many subtle benefits to the soil, including to its microbial integrity. These benefits are perceptible only after careful observation of soil structure or ecological interactions over decades or generations, or else after using sophisticated equipment. Only knowledge of how wind, weeds and water interact with the sun and soil will allow one to appreciate fully the benefits of so-called lazy beds.

Almost the entire landscape in parts of Ireland is corduroyed with them, and while the most clearly defined ridges are likely to date from the decades leading up to the Famine, when the population skyrocketed in the eighteenth and nineteenth centuries, there are other, fainter ridges that appear as ghostly apparitions when the sun is low in the sky or when a frost or light snow lies on the ground. These are the remains of ridges that archaeologists have found can date from the Bronze Age, and even in some cases to when Neolithic farmers brought basic agricultural techniques here six thousand years ago.

The practice continued as each generation of farmer over the millennia came to realise how ideally suited ridges were to the specific conditions of shallow mineral soils and a wet climate.

The most remarkable thing about the lazy beds is that they are still clearly visible despite more than a century and a half of tractors and quads driving over them, not to mention the hooves of cattle, sheep and horses, the claws of dogs and foxes and the hobnailed, hiking and wellington boots of humans. This is also their most poignant aspect, as the reason they have held their form is not only that they were dug and dug again for so many years but also that many of them were never dug up after the final time they were shaped and planted in the 1840s. By the time the crop was ready in that final year, either the people had died or emigrated or they were too weak to dig them. Or else they noticed the blight-rotted stems and knew there would be nothing but a slimy mush beneath the soil. The lines are now memorials of the desperation that comes when you realise that a monocultural and unsustainable way of farming that has served and nourished you for years suddenly fails.

I can appreciate the powerful impact of this, but then I also find myself going to great lengths to avoid feeling the full consequences of it. The brain finds it hard to face up to such tragedy, so it conspires to create clever avoidance strategies. We dismiss the thought as being something from the distant past, or we even deny it outright. It's easier that way, and yet recent neuro-psychiatric research points to the negative repercussions of ignoring past trauma.

We now know that it doesn't vanish: it festers. Epigenetic study is also revealing how our bodies hold on to the trauma of past generations. The memories are not only in the national consciousness but also in our cellular structure too – in our internal organs and our nervous system. There's no point hiding from something that is already within us.

In the light of this, we might as well start to address this pain in our past. Ultimately, things will become clearer and easier if we do. We can begin to understand why our people are known as heavy drinkers throughout the world. We can come to appreciate why we fail to learn Irish in schools, despite the vast sums the Government has spent on its promotion for almost a century. We might stop blaming our failure to learn on teachers, or the education system, or Government policy, and realise that we have no difficulty learning any other subject in school – subjects that are taught by the same teachers, using the same methods.

Only by coming to terms with the Famine can we finally start to acknowledge, and maybe even address, the deep psychological block within us that prevents us from learning the language and respecting the land.

We'll recognise the neural pathways and thought patterns that prevent the language taking hold in our minds and that alienated us from our traditional respect for the land.

The one certainty shared by everyone who suffered during the Famine was that there was no certainty for them any longer. There was no future. Once the crops had failed year after year, they lost faith in the ability of the soil to feed them. Nature had abandoned them. They believed that the only option for their children and themselves was escape – to emigrate to the cities, or even to the United States or England or Australia, and for that they needed English. So it was a mix of parental love and the survival instinct common to all creatures that made parents insist that their children wouldn't speak Irish. English was the future; Irish would bring only further suffering and death.

It had long been believed in England that the only way to fully subjugate the nation was to eradicate the Irish language. Accordingly, the national school system had been introduced a decade before, in 1831, to help catalyse this by making it clear that English was the language of progress and that the speaking of Irish was punishable by beating.

Many of the original national school buildings from 1831 are extant, as are famine roads and walls built in return for food rations. Extant too are the workhouses they sought shelter in, the famine pits in which they were buried and the abandoned villages they left behind. The landscape can help concentrate our minds on all these things once we are ready to address them. It's not easy to do: such physical relics can shorten the gap between that time and this in unsettling ways. But by bringing us closer to the trauma, they help speed up the healing and ultimately salve the hungry ghosts of our ancestors.

The most visible of these earth remnants, at least in the west of Ireland, are famine roads, stone-built tracks that wander aimlessly through the landscape. They are roads without function, built to bring people to where no one would ever want to go. Sometimes they zigzag up a mountain, or across a bog, or out onto an abandoned promontory. They almost always come to a sudden halt at nothing in particular. They are like scars on the landscape from a series of violent attacks.

They are the result of labour schemes imposed under the strictures of the Poor Law, which insisted that any alms offered would be in return for work. This was considered a means to dissuade the 'undeserving poor' from what was believed to be their inherently parasitic behaviour. Initially, it was thought that the schemes would focus on bringing the vast stretches of unproductive bog into cultivation, but it was decided instead to opt for purposeless projects, such as building needless roads or futile follies so that landlords couldn't benefit from the schemes.

It's difficult to understand why the British government, instead of simply feeding them, made people who were already weakened by starvation expend precious reserves on toiling on pointless projects for food. By 1846 more than half a million starving men, women and children were employed in the construction of stone roads and other follies such as piers in the middle of bogs, whimsical buildings and towering estate walls. At its peak, 700,000 Irish people were devoted full time to the construction of useless infrastructure in often appalling weather, with inadequate tools and not enough food. Oftentimes, the money they were supposed to receive was delayed, and the people were scammed by corrupt officials and landlords.

It can be hard for us now to look at these features, often in the most picturesque regions of the Wild Atlantic Way, such as in Dunquin on the Dingle Peninsula, or in Clifden, or around Killary Harbour in Co. Mayo, and imagine the desperate men, women and children smashing up rocks and carrying the rubble to construction sites.

I've only once driven along the spectacular Healy Pass across the Beara Peninsula from Adrigole in Co. Cork to Lauragh in Co. Kerry because I found the whole experience harrowing. It's a wild, serpentine strip of tarmac through a remote and desolate landscape that loops seemingly endlessly around the sinuous contours of the peaks of Stookeennalackareha (Stuaicín na Leaca Réidhe, literally 'pinnacle of the smooth hillside'), Claddaghgarriff (An Cladach Garbh, 'rough heap of stones') and Knockanouganish (Cnoc an Uaignis, 'hill of loneliness') in the Caha mountain range. At the top of the pass is a stone known as the Flat Rock, where coffins were rested by mourners who would make their way uphill from one county to be met by those from the other county, who would carry the body down the other side.

The panoramic views along the road are spectacular, with Bantry Bay, Glenmore Lake and the Kenmare River stretching out below; and yet it's hard not to think back to the year it was built, 1847, when it was planned as one of the few Famine projects that had a purpose: to unite the communities in Co. Cork and Co. Kerry separated by the mountain range. I was torn between revelling in the beauty and imagining the people who died during its construction. These were the less-well-off fellow county folk of my own Co. Kerry ancestors. Their blood and suffering had created the road, and it was hard to get beyond this.

WORKHOUSES

Perhaps the most obvious and dominating legacy of the Famine on the landscape is the workhouse. These are institutional block buildings built between 1838 and 1841 to house the destitute. They weren't really prisons, as inmates were free to leave; but they had high walls, and people went there only as a last resort, as it was believed that one rarely came out alive. Sadly, this was often the case. The cramped conditions, poor hygiene and inadequate medical care meant that diseases were rife.

Whole families had to enter together to make it easier for landlords to clear the land of tenants. Once they were inside, children were separated from their parents and segregated according to sex, sometimes never seeing their parents or siblings again. During the height of the Famine, all 130 workhouses in the country were crammed with destitute people, and a further 33 workhouses were built.

People risked contracting the rampant diseases inside in return for two meals a day that often consisted of gruel-like stirabout, with milk and potatoes. All inmates had to work for their food and board, with men breaking stones for building roads. Women and children walked endlessly in circles pushing a large wheel used for grinding corn. The specific jobs varied depending on the workhouse. Older inmates were set to spinning wool or mending clothes or picking oakum, which involved separating out strands of old ships' rope to be reused as caulking. Much of the work was unproductive: one of the rules was that workhouses couldn't compete with outside businesses. Women were also meant to be trained for domestic service, but this mainly involved their cleaning and cooking for the workhouse.

The fear that these places instilled in communities is still palpable today. At a deep level, we haven't forgotten the approximately 200,000 people who died within them during the Famine years. The Kilkenny workhouse had 4,357 inmates at its peak, whereas it was built to house a maximum of 1,300. When typhus hit Co. Kilkenny, the results were predictable: people died in large numbers, and when the local cemeteries banned pauper burials, the workhouse guardians had to start digging mass graves inside their own grounds. Archaeologists who excavated the site in 2014 estimated that each pit had about a week's worth of bodies in it. They were stacked one on top of the other in a single hole.

Conditions in workhouses were harsh and the treatment of inmates was intentionally cruel to discourage people from entering the place and also to encourage those inside to leave as soon as possible. The aim of the Poor Law was that inmates should be 'worse fed, worse clothed and worse lodged than the independent labourers of the district'.[†] There was often violence, with inmates causing trouble in the hope of being transferred to prison, where the food was better and the regime less strict.

Still today, the elderly in most towns and villages can tell you where the local workhouse was, because they didn't just disappear after the Famine years. They continued right up until Ireland gained its independence, as the principal refuge for society's supposed misfits: unmarried mothers, impoverished families, the elderly and infirm, children born outside marriage, 'vagrants' with mild mental disabilities and orphaned and abandoned children.

After the Famine there were up to 120,000 children without any surviving family sheltering in workhouses.

† J.G. Kohl, *Ireland, England, and Scotland* (London: Chapman and Hall, 1844), p. 155.

In theory, they were supposed to receive an education, but the teachers were poorly trained and unsympathetic and couldn't cope with enormous classes of traumatised, hungry children. An English cleric described the children in the Limerick workhouse as skeletons covered in sores and dressed in rags. Social reformers encouraged the authorities to allow families to foster the children, but they made slow progress. Eventually, in the 1870s, religious orders set up industrial schools, in which children were meant to receive training and religious instruction. Yet by the beginning of the twentieth century one in seven of the almost 42,000 workhouse inmates were still children.

The industrial schools, of course, went on to become another realm of torture for young boys and girls – institutions that still bring darkness to their environment. They joined the workhouses as edifices of fear and shame. And the workhouses continued their impact on the nation. In the 1920s, 33 of them became county homes, offering relief to the elderly and chronic invalids; 32 became district or fever hospitals; and 9 became county hospitals. Many others were damaged when occupied by soldiers during the War of Independence and the Civil War. However, either as medical buildings or as ruins, they persisted in the landscape, and even today ten of them still stand, three of which have been converted into museums.

I remember visiting an old woman on her deathbed in the gaunt, decrepit workhouse building that had become the local hospital in Dingle. She had been reared on the Blasket Islands and forcibly relocated to the mainland in the 1950s. She had always seemed invincible in her heavy tweed skirt and thick-stockinged legs as she chased the gander and the cockerel up the yard. But as I visited her with my grandmother in the former workhouse that day, she appeared haunted and harrowed. She kept repeating that she had no fear of death and was looking forward to meeting Ár Máthair Síor-Chabhrach ('Our Mother of Perpetual Succour'). All she wanted was to escape that building as soon as she could. I hadn't understood at the time because, although the ward was a bit drab, it seemed clean and the nurses were friendly.

It was only on the way home that my grandmother explained that the hospital had once been the workhouse and that still then, in the 1980s, the top storey remained unchanged since those dark days. It was one vast plank-floored dormitory with raised wooden platforms on which the inmates slept on straw or reeds. The walls were still grimy and peeling with damp, and the original iron beds that the Sisters of Mercy had bought in the late nineteenth century in an attempt to improve conditions were now stored up there.

No wonder the old woman was haunted: she would have been hearing all her life of the many generations of her family and neighbours who had suffered and died in *teach na mbocht* ('the poor house'), as it was known. At one point, one in every seven people on the Dingle Peninsula was an inmate there or in the stables and store-houses that were used as auxiliary workhouses nearby. Many hundreds of these starving people now lie without headstones in a rough undulating field of mounds and hummocks just behind the workhouse.

I have tried to get inside the building to see the top floor for myself, but the hospital closed in 2010, and the health authority has it locked up, with surveillance day and night. There are, though, other workhouses that have been preserved as museums, including ones in Portumna in Co. Galway, Donaghmore in Co. Laois and Limavady in Co. Derry, as well as many others that have been extensively altered, such as in Dunfanaghy in Co. Donegal, or allowed fall into decline, as in Bawnboy in Co. Cavan.

There are still quite a few hospitals with elements of the original workhouse intact. Naas General Hospital has been so modernised that no trace of the original building remains except the three acres of Famine burial ground behind the hospital, but there are still a few outbuildings at Skibbereen Community Hospital from its time as a workhouse and a high forbidding perimeter wall that was used to keep starving local people out – those who, according to accounts of the time, would often walk and crawl from up to twenty miles away in the hope of receiving food. They were often sent away with nothing.

The hospital at Skibbereen has an old Famine burial ground too, but at the height of the Famine there were just too many bodies every day, and so a death cart would leave the workhouse every morning carrying bodies to a mass grave three kilometres away on the banks of the River Ilen. This burial ground is part of another tragic network of Famine-related features in the landscape, namely grave pits and mass burial sites. Again, if you ask around in any area, local people will point out where the victims of the Famine were buried, and they'll probably have stories about family members interred there too.

SKIBBEREEN

The mass burial site at Skibbereen is known as Abbeystrowry Cemetery. The workhouse doctor at the time of the Famine, Dan Donovan, published accounts of his experience in the Cork-based *Southern Reporter* newspaper. He noted that they had 'a public coffin, a public cart, and a man employed every day who is paid one shilling per head to convey the dead only to one graveyard called The Abbey'. He saw the burial ground as being like 'a battlefield, pyramids of coffins piled on each other. Naked corpses protruding from the ground. And large pits dug.'

Today the graveyard is on the side of the main N71 road to Ballydehob, and visiting it is a sobering experience. There are medieval ruins of a Franciscan priory, nineteenth-century wrought-iron crosses, and ornate headstones, but what really gets under your skin is the bare, lumpy patch of undulating grass near the entrance. Its unassuming appearance belies the fact that nine thousand victims of starvation and disease lie beneath it.

Seeing it brings to mind Dr Donovan's description of the

> legions of half-naked, starving people parading the streets from morning to night, and in every direction nothing but misery, the most extreme, is to be witnessed.

He described the rotting bodies he saw in many houses, how dogs and pigs would feed on them and how the appearance of people all around him would change as they stopped eating.

> In a short time the face and limbs become frightfully emaciated; the eyes acquire a most peculiar stare; the skin exhaled a peculiar and offensive foetor, and was covered with a brownish, filthy-looking coating, almost as indelible as varnish.

It's hard not to get a sense of the loss and the unresolved trauma that persists in such places. In an account published in 1874, Canon John O'Rourke noted that

> immediately inside the gate, a little to the right, are those monster graves called by the people 'the pits' into which the dead were thrown coffinless in hundreds, without mourning or ceremony hurried away by stealth, frequently at the dead of night, to elude observation and to enable the survivors to attend public works next day and thus prolong for a while their unequal contest with the all-conquering famine.

An entire generation of Skibbereen people, O'Rourke wrote, were buried there within a year and a half.

There's another account by a young Oxford student, Frederick Temple Hamilton-Temple-Blackwood, who went on to become Lord Dufferin, governor-general of Canada. In 1847, at the age of 21, he travelled to Skibbereen and wrote that there was

> about an acre of uneven and freshly-turned earth ... allotted to the late victims of the famine and disease; by these graves, no service had been performed, no friends had stood, no priest had spoken words of hope and of future

consolation in a glorious eternity. The bodies had been daily thrown in, many without a coffin, one over another, the uppermost only hidden from the light of day by a bare three inches of earth, the survivors not even knowing the spot where those most dear to them lay sleeping.

There are many similar accounts of conditions in the country, but the problem is that few of us, apart from historians, ever read them. These accounts can help bring alive for us what happened in the land. Then, by visiting the sites, we can further awaken the past and begin the process of resolution.

The grave sites are almost everywhere you turn in Ireland. Just a short distance to the west, in the harbour town of Schull, Dr Donovan observed that

the formalities of making a regular grave is scarcely complied with; a deep hole is dug, and men commit the bodies of their friends and relatives to the earth with less ceremony than would some time ago be bestowed on a favourite dog; not even a mound of clay is raised to mark the spot.

A bit further west again, in Dunmanus,

coffinless bodies are interred in numbers at night, and as the soil is light, heaps of stones are laid over them to prevent the starving dogs that are roaming around the country from devouring the human remains.

Poignantly, Dr Donovan talks about the psychological effects on people and about how the 'ardent domestic affections of the Irish peasant' have been quashed.

The funeral cry is now never heard; children look upon the death struggle of their parents without apparent sorrow and mothers see their offspring die without shedding tears.

A woman who had five sick children

would think myself lucky if they were all dead before morning … This time twelve-months I would as soon lose my heart's blood as one of my children, but it is killing me now to see them starving, and to hear them crying.

And everywhere around him, Dr Donavan would see

women wrap the bodies of their deceased children in cloths, take them to the places of interment themselves, and consign them to the graves without the assistance of a single friend. The once warm-hearted people never now enter the hovels where death has laid low his victim; and corpses are not removed until the factor of decomposition compels the weak and sick to make an effort beyond their strength to perform for deceased friends the last sad office which many of themselves are destined soon to require.

The scenes of mass burial that Hamilton-Temple-Blackwood witnessed in 1847 were reduced significantly after 1848, but in December 1849 there were still one hundred Famine victims a week being buried in Abbeystrowry. Even then, many burials were taking place at night, with people burying their dead in secret, too ashamed to be seen doing so without a coffin or shroud, or too afraid to have it known that fever had entered their dwelling. The district around Skibbereen lost 36 per cent of its population between 1841 and 1851. Over a third of family, friends and neighbours were wiped out.

These are the memories held by the traumatised ghosts of our ancestors that need to be released. It is in no way easy to reflect on such things, and yet our future connection with this land and with the legacy of our own heritage requires us to come to terms with it so that we can begin the process of properly grieving, honouring the suffering and resolving to move beyond it. It's a familiar and almost intuitive process that we learnt first as toddlers when told to face up to hurts and then to try to forgive the person or thing that had inflicted them on us. And for us now, as a people in an island territory that was once a beacon of light in the world, it is vital if we wish to return to our former glory.

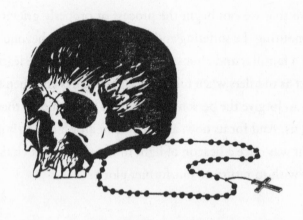

CILLÍNÍ

Flying into Co. Donegal is a powerful experience. On a fine day, one dips down from the clouds into a spectacular scene of indigo Atlantic waters turning aquamarine as they approach the golden shores. Stretching out in both directions are pale sandy beaches, dark granite rocks and tiny craggy islands, with the purple-blue Derryveagh Mountains in the distance and the soaring peak of Mount Errigal beyond. Fields of lime, olive, ochre and russet clad the land, peppered with weather-rounded rocks and broad lichen-stained flagstones. It's no surprise that this tiny airport has been voted the World's Most Scenic three years running, beating off competition from Tanzania, Fiji and French Polynesia.

The great expanses of Glenveigh National Park are the primary lure in the area, but I find myself often following the golden line of Carrickfin Beach, which runs parallel with the runway to a white-sanded cove barricaded by a tall rocky outcrop. The rock is just like any other along the coast here, except that it's topped by thin soil and tough, wind-bitten salt-burnt grass. When the tide is in, the rock becomes an island known as Illannamarve, from the Irish Oileán na Marbh ('Island of the Dead'), a name that makes you stop and pause.

It was the fisherman, Donnchadh Ó Baoill, who first pointed it out to me, describing it as a tragic spot, a place of past trauma. Illannamarve, he said, was where local people would bury their stillborn and unbaptised babies when the Church forbade them from using the consecrated ground of graveyards.

Denying the bereaved the consolation of an honourable burial seems particularly cruel and vindictive, and yet this was the norm in the past few centuries during which the Church managed to exert maximum control over the people. It led to the existence of unofficial burial grounds, called *cillíní*, *cealdracha* or *ceallúnaigh*, which can be found throughout the country. There are more than 1,400 documented on official maps but many multiples more were probably never recorded.

Even into the 1930s seven children out of every hundred died in their first year of life. It was just an inevitable part of existence, and since the Church turned its back on these unfortunate babies and parents, people had no option but to dig a hole at night in some obscure spot. It was considered a shameful act because losing a baby was regarded as a punishment on the mother by a vengeful God.

And it wasn't just babies who died in childbirth, or shortly after, who were buried in these *cillíní*. There were others too, such as victims of infanticide: infants born to parents unable or unwilling to care for them in an era before contraception or state adoption services. It must be stressed that this occurred mostly after the Middle Ages, when Gaelic society had been so debased by oppression that desperate measures were needed. Before that, fosterage and adoption were a central part of tribal life, stretching back as far as the Iron Age and possibly into the Bronze Age.

An elderly crab fisherman in Annagary told me that when out checking his pots at night as a young man he'd occasionally see grieving mothers or disconsolate fathers carrying tiny bundles and a spade out across the strand to Illannamarve at low tide. He'd pretend not to see them, but everyone knew what was happening.

Each townland had some isolated spot where babies were buried, but in the past, whenever I'd ask in rural areas about the practice, people would find a way to avoid answering. It was still a shameful secret. Not mentioning it was easier than unearthing and confronting the trauma and tragedy. But memories lingered not only within the minds of people but possibly within the land itself. Buried beneath the briars, blackthorn bushes and rushes were resonances of suffering.

Now, finally, it is becoming easier to talk about such things, and it can be worthwhile asking older people about *cillín* sites in their area because it helps bring some of the darkness into the light. However, this can still be a sore subject for those who may have a baby brother or sister buried there, unacknowledged, in the wasteland.

The *cillín* was often situated on liminal land, far from the main areas of activity. It stemmed from the belief that boundary regions were beyond the normal rules and restrictions of society. It's why the bog bodies are more often found along the thresholds of different kingdoms. In the same way, you'll find *cillíní* on the seashore, like Illannamarve, or on a lake shore, or on the boundaries of a townland, or at a crossroads. Occasionally, they'll be tucked away in the corner of a distant field or in a scrap of worthless boggy or wooded land.

The Church always occupied central locations, so the *cillíní* were relegated to the margins. In fact, the most common locations were abandoned archaeological sites, such as ring forts or the ruins of early ecclesiastical buildings. These were chosen as appropriate burial places in the hope that some of the sanctity of the original pagan or Early Christian site might still linger there.

Their liminality wasn't just to help hide the shame: it was to confuse and contain the uneasy spirits interred within, who, it was felt, were less likely to cross territorial boundaries or confront the supernatural spirits that lingered in such places. The hope was that the souls of the babies would rest easier in these forgotten margins and were less likely to haunt the living.

Of the *cillíní* recorded by the state, more than a quarter are in Co. Galway, and another sixth of them are in Co. Kerry. Their profusion in these less fertile western counties is possibly due to the higher rate of infant mortality there and to the fact that the poorer land meant that the *cillíní* were less likely to be disturbed by intensive farming and suburban sprawl. Some eastern counties, such as Louth and Westmeath, have only a couple of *cillín* sites left, but the likelihood is that there would have been scores of them in every county at one time. And the psychological impact of the trauma the *cillíní* represent lingers even though they may have been ploughed back into the land or covered in concrete decades ago.

As we know, the land of Ireland is no stranger to death. There've been battles and massacres throughout the ages, not to mention the all-too-frequent famines that purged the population in the 1330s, 1520s, 1650s, 1740s,

1840s and 1870s when crops failed or weather destroyed everything. All left a legacy of decomposing bodies in their wake. It's the innocence of the unbaptised babies buried in the *cillíní* that set them apart and that led people to respect the sites and not interfere with them. They were safe and undisturbed in their isolated patches – at least until our culture became so disconnected from our past that many of the threads binding us to the old customs were severed.

Even so, if you visit the strand at Carnboy that leads out to Illannamarve today, you'll rarely see local families swimming there. They tend to go elsewhere, recognising and respecting the legacy of the place.

In all my visits to Co. Donegal, I had never set foot on Illannamarve until filming a television series on peatlands in 2021. The tide was in when I reached Carnboy, so I had to swim across the small bay with my glasses tucked into my togs so that I could see things when I reached the island. It was a bright August afternoon and the water was tropical blue, with the marram grass warm underfoot. However, the knowledge that there were more than five hundred bodies buried in the sparse soil beneath me still sent a chill up my spine as I climbed the tiny island.

It's possible that there weren't only babies buried there, as *cillíní* were often used to dispose of unwanted outsiders too: wandering strangers, foreign sailors, excommunicates and the severely disabled. Sometimes criminals and murder victims were also deposited, but it wasn't common.

That the bodies were left undisturbed has inadvertently helped the discipline of archaeology, as the historical features among which they were buried were preserved alongside them. This is particularly true of ring forts, which are often the remains of early medieval homesteads, with a circular bank surrounding them to keep domestic animals in and to protect livestock from wolves and animal rustlers. The belief that these forts were the dwelling places of fairies who would wreak vengeance if disturbed has helped preserve many ring forts (often known as 'fairy forts'). It's possible that the entire mythology of fairies living in ring forts was devised simply to ensure that the resting places of the community's babies were left undisturbed. And the extension of the *fóidín mearaí*, the stray sod that sent people awry when they stood on it, to include places associated with the burial sites of babies was potentially another ploy to keep people from trespassing on these hallowed grounds.

One final point of interest is that most *cillíní* are not very old. Almost all date from the post-medieval and early modern period, when the old honour code of Gaelic society had crumbled and people had become so downtrodden that they had to resort to the inhumane strictures imposed on them by the clergy.

The Church may have made earlier attempts to prohibit the unbaptised from being buried in grave-yards, but only in the seventeenth century do we find a definitive reference to a *cillín* in a letter referring to the reuse of an old graveyard in Co. Donegal 'as a burial-place for unbaptised children and suicides'. From then on, *cillíní* were part of mainstream culture, until the arcane and judgemental teachings surrounding purgatory were relaxed as part of Vatican II reforms in the 1960s. However, it does seem that some *cillíní* were used right up to the 1980s.

Thankfully, the tradition is entirely ended now, though the risk is that the *cillíní* could be forgotten entirely, becoming overgrown with brambles or being ploughed up for the sake of agricultural intensification. It would be a shame to allow this to happen, at least until we have had a chance to acknowledge what had happened in them over the last few centuries and to make our peace with the legacy of it.

RING FORTS

There's a lot more to be said about ring forts than just their role as burial places for unbaptised babies. They are primarily the remains of ancient homesteads. And since the old roads, ritual sites and cultivation beds of our ancestors still survive in the land, it's no surprise that their homes do too. Seek out a high vantage point in any part of the island and you're likely to see grass-covered banks in the shape of a perfect circle somewhere in the landscape, or a clump of trees or bushes in a field that form the perimeter of a neat circle. The likelihood is that these are ring forts, the most common form of one-off housing and defensive outpost in Ireland from the Late

Iron Age right through early Christianity and up to the Middle Ages.

These circular embankments are all that remain of the defensive structures that would have surrounded the farmsteads and lookout forts of our pastoral ancestors. The houses would have been built out of a mix of timber and wattle-and-daub (which would have long since decayed back into the soil) or stone that might later have been reused elsewhere, so that only the outer perimeter survives. In parts of the west of Ireland where timber was scarce and where there wasn't even enough soil to berm up into an embankment, they used rocks and stones for everything, and these homesteads are called *caisil* ('cashels'). They were the homes, gathering places, defensive forts and workshops of a particular tribe or an extended family.

Think of them as fortified ranches, surrounded by one or more ditches and banks, which would often have been crowned by a wooden palisade to keep livestock in and wolves and raiders out. More than 32,000 of them survive in the landscape today, which is an impressive number considering that most date from between the sixth and tenth centuries. It was within these spaces that the household would have slept, prepared food and gathered for social occasions with neighbours and wider family. Here is also where they planned raids, embroidered textiles, sifted seeds, sang songs, played board games and shared meals around a central fireplace. The law tracts of the seventh and eighth centuries offer a good sense of their construction and size, as well as of the activities that happened within them.

Their ubiquity is best visualised by the Twitterbot and Instagram feed @everyringfort, which posts a satellite image of a different ring fort every hour. The man behind it, Keith Ó Faoláin, began isolating images from satellite maps using a text-character recognition algorithm in March 2019 and has used this automated data-mining process to keep posting images of different sites hourly, day and night, continuously ever since. It will continue to do so until May 2023, so that you can have your days and years marked out by a different unit of measurement than hours and days. The declining duration of your time on the planet can be counted in the form of early medieval Irish homesteads.

Once you begin receiving these ring forts hourly in your social media streams, you'll start to see them everywhere in the landscape too, and you will begin to appreciate how they differ from each other, mostly in size, but in shape too, as occasionally additional compounds will be built onto the side of the circle, or two circles might be joined to form a figure of eight. The raised boundary of a modest homestead could be as small as ten metres in diameter, while a chief's or a noble's residence might be seventy metres wide, with multiple banks to encircle the homes, stores, workshops and meeting places within.

Their size dictates the status not only of the original inhabitants but also of the supernatural beings that were later believed to occupy them. The more prominent the ring fort, the more elevated the fairy in residence – so a large ring fort might be home not only to run-of-the-mill fairies but to an actual king or queen of the fairies in a particular region.

These Otherworldly beings have now become a central component of ring forts – or at least they were until recently. It was widely believed that ring forts – or *ráthanna* or *liosanna* in Irish – were entrances to the Otherworld, where Tuatha Dé Danann retreated when our forebears invaded the island. That many had underground, or souterrain, passages burrowing into the earth made this idea all the more credible, although these passages rarely proceeded very deeply and are now understood to have been used for storage, for providing refuge or as a clandestine escape route during an attack.

To get a sense of how pervasive the link between ring forts and fairies is, consider the hundreds of accounts of magical occurrences at ring forts documented in the Schools' Collection.[†] Still today, every county has endless stories of Otherworldly activities in local ring forts. My mother is convinced that she saw a leprechaun in the ring fort behind the family house in Corca Dhuibhne, and

† Accessible at https://www.duchas.ie/en/cbes.

I've heard it claimed with absolute conviction that the demise of Seán Quinn's cement and insurance empire in Co. Cavan in 2011 and of John DeLorean's sports car industry in Belfast in 1982 were directly attributable to the conscious destruction of 'sacred' ring forts during the construction of these sites.

The M18 motorway from Galway to Limerick was rerouted twenty years ago after a local *seanchaí* and historian, Eddie Lenihan, pointed out in the *Irish Times* that a local *sceach*, or fairy bush, was an important sacred site considered to be a meeting place for the fairy hordes of Connacht and Munster in many folk tales. Fairy bushes were often associated with ring forts, as the *sceach* (hawthorn) is the most likely plant to grow on an abandoned bit of well-drained land. Lenihan warned that if the bush were destroyed during the construction of the motorway, the fairies might retaliate by causing road accidents. The claims were picked up by the *New York Times* and CNN, which appears to have led Transport Infrastructure Ireland (formerly the National Roads Authority) to divert the road around it. The county roads engineer insisted to me that this never happened, and yet if you stand on the overpass at Junction 10 you can clearly see how the route kinks slightly to the east to avoid the bush, which stands proudly between the northbound lane and the on-ramp on the western side.

It was this connection that ring forts had to fairies, as well as the tradition of using them as places of rest for unbaptised babies, that helped ensure their survival for so long. Alas, as we find ourselves increasingly disconnected from the stories of the landscape, more ring forts are beginning to be ploughed under by farmers under pressure from financial lenders and industrial farming interests to maximise the yield on every inch of their land. Excavators have become almost as common as tractors in fields in recent years, and it's only a morning's work to flatten out an earthen bank that may have existed for a millennium or more. Since ring forts were first surveyed in the nineteenth century, about ten thousand have been destroyed.

That said, most farmers do still respect them and go to great trouble to leave the banks undisturbed and avoid cutting the *sceacha* that grow on them, as these are considered to have magical properties. Sadly, it's more often the Government that destroys ring forts these days while building roads or facilitating the development of industrial infrastructure. Transport Infrastructure Ireland boasted that in just one road project alone, the N9/M10 Kilcullen to Waterford scheme, fifty-four archaeological sites were uncovered, dug and then paved over. Considering that ring forts are the second most plentiful archaeological feature in the country, it's safe to assume that a large proportion of these features were ring forts.

Clearly, every ring fort cannot be regarded as a sacred historic monument and left untouched for ever, and yet more than twenty thousand archaeological licences to excavate have been issued by the state in the past twenty years. The vast majority were excavations financed by the state for road construction, and in most instances only a thin strip of the site gets excavated before the entirety is removed by diggers so that the road, or other major development, can proceed. We should at least bear in mind that every step towards 'progress' involves obliterating more of our past.

In theory, ring forts are classified as national monuments and are therefore protected by the state, but this protection is now being revoked regularly by the Government in the course of its construction of new infrastructure. In fact, the National Monuments (Amendment) Act (2004) changed the legislation to further empower the state to demolish any newly discovered national monument on any motorway route, without an in-depth environmental impact assessment. This has been used extensively ever since.

This focus on unbridled financial and industrial development at the expense of heritage and environmental cohesion has had a heavy impact on the landscape. Not only are EU monitoring bodies continually chiding the Government for its failure to protect the country's environmental ecosystems, but the European Court of

Justice and other courts have often ruled against our narrow and biased interpretation of environmental impact assessment directives in relation to archaeological heritage sites.

It's always a tricky balance between conserving the old and making room for the new, but often it seems that the Government relies on our poor understanding of the importance and uniqueness of what is around us and beneath us to push through its agenda. It's regrettable because, as we've seen, the land has much it wants to communicate with us, and much it can teach us. It's natural that we would have turned against it when it failed to feed our people through those awful years in the 1840s. But we are now far enough away from that wound to reassess things and to begin to build a renewed relationship, harmony and partnership with our patch of rocky island. It's vital that we don't destroy it before we get to know it again.

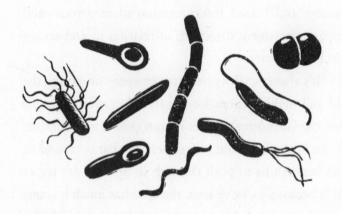

RESONANCE

It should be clear now how meaningful and complex our surroundings are. We're part of a planet that seeded us, human beings, who are now entirely dependent on it. Our bodies sprang from the earth and are still in constant communication with it in complex and bewildering ways. In the air we breathe, the water we drink and the food we eat, we are intrinsically connected with it. Not to mention the bacteria, fungi, protozoa and viruses living on and inside our bodies and which outnumber our human cells ten to one. Collectively these are known as our microbiome and they are in absolute unity with the land. They cannot be separated. We are the land.

Scientists are now beginning to reveal the interconnectivity of humans and landscape in countless ways, including how energy waves emitted by the planet in the form of magnetic radiation affect human health and behaviour. There are even now studies showing that magnetic forces that are released by the earth, the sun and the planets appear to be a catalyst for incidents of social unrest and major global events.

The Soviet astrophysicist Alexander Chizhevsky in the 1940s charted increases in solar activity from the mid-eighteenth century onwards and found that they seem to correspond with uncanny accuracy to commencements of wars, uprisings and other dramatic shifts in humanity. The lines on a graph charting these two elements over the last few centuries and right up to the present day run parallel to each other. Correlation should never be confused with causation, but there does appear to be strong links between the two.

It's known that sun flares relating to increased solar activity cause fluctuations in the earth's magnetic field, and according to research at the HeartMath Institute in Boulder Creek, California, this then appears to affect our health and behaviour. The institute claims that bursts of human creativity correlate with increased solar activity. In short, the sun helps us flourish, which is no surprise to anyone – certainly not to the builders of the many sun-oriented ritual sites or to the myth-makers who first described how Ireland's iconic warrior figure Cú Chulainn was formed through a union of a sun king, a god of light and an earth goddess.

Scientists working at the HeartMath Institute have established a network of ultrasensitive magnetic field detectors throughout the planet that continually monitor fluctuations in the earth's geomagnetic fields alongside resonances in the ionosphere. They then track how they correspond to changes in human heart variability and other biological factors. Magnetometers that measure the strength and direction of magnetic fields on or near the earth have been installed in Africa, South America, Canada, Japan, Europe, Malaysia, Saudi Arabia and New Zealand to continually track the changes in geomagnetic activity caused by solar storms, changes in solar wind speed and disruption of the Schumann resonance, which consists of extremely low-frequency (ELF) electromagnetic resonances in the ionosphere caused by global lightning discharges.

Base stations spread over each continent send back results of the resonance frequencies they record to a central hub, which then converts this into a real-time picture of the earth's shifting rhythms or pulse. The science of this is beyond my comprehension, but their findings appear to show that the earth is continuously emitting information that the human body then responds to.

It will take further study and more sophisticated apparatus to reveal whether the great gathering sites of Ireland that have been attracting followers for thousands of years are emitting frequencies that most of us are no longer conscious of, or whether the mysterious solar alignments that were laid out between significant points in prehistory by our Neolithic and Bronze Age forebears are part of an energy or magnetic grid that we have forgotten how to decipher. What does seem clear, though, is that our world and all the beings and plants within it are elements of a biofeedback loop, in which all of us are intermingled in innumerable ways.

It can help to bear in mind how indigenous communities relate to their landscape and how they discuss the two-way communication that occurs between them and the land. For many, the past lies embedded in features of the earth, in rivers, canyons, mountains, rocks and lakes. As the Apache elder Nick Thompson has said, 'white men need paper maps. We have maps in our minds.'† The land can communicate with us and shape how we think.

Knowledge of place becomes the basis of self-knowledge. Without it we find it much harder to grasp our position in the larger scheme of things, including our own communities. The Kiowa elder N. Scott Momaday has said that the Native American person is 'deeply invested in the earth, committed to it both in his consciousness and in his instinct. Only in reference to the earth can he persist in his identity.'

† Keith H. Basso, *Wisdom Sits in Places: Landscape and Language among the Western Apache* (Albuquerque, N. Mex.: University of New Mexico Press, 1996).

Our way of describing the history of Ireland is now distant and unfamiliar. It's no longer in the songs and stories of the people, being now confined to the printed page and to academia. It's disconnected from the soil, and by focusing so exclusively on logical, linear thought it misses so much. It is history without voices or energy – history without soul or spirit to thrust it into the present. The historical journal has its place and is extremely valuable, as long as it is combined with walking and feeling the earth, and ideally also with an immersion in the mythology.

Only by combining all these elements can we get a true picture of who we are, where we came from and what directions we might dare to proceed in from here. It is up to us now to go out and walk the land, to rediscover our surroundings and reimagine our place in the world.

Place names can be an important tool to help us with this. We must get over the idea that they are merely words used to refer to specific places: they can reveal much more than that. Often, they convey something of the tribes, warriors and mythical gods who inhabited the landscape. They remind us that the land is an enchanted place where wonders once happened, where nature once thrived, and that soil is more than where profit can be accrued. The PR companies so handsomely paid by property developers to name their housing complexes need to bear this in mind.

Our concept of our tribal past and the sense of ourselves today are intertwined with our sense of place. This is clear from how the mythical tales focus almost as much on where events occurred as on the events themselves. Navajo and Apache cultures believe that if narrated events aren't spatially anchored, their significance is somehow reduced, making them less open to proper assessment. It isn't just a matter of lending life and veracity to a tale: projecting the narrative events onto the landscape animates them, adding dimensions and means of engagement. We're fortunate in Ireland that our topography still has multiple layers of historical and mythical significance that can enrich our existence – as long as we can still access and decipher it.

The prime focus and motivator that formed the basis of so many of the outlandish mythical stories is the goddess, who is a representative of the land itself. The many forms she takes are a reflection of the myriad forms of landscape and the natural world; but what all her personas point to is that all life is interconnected – plant, animal, human and spirit. That's why humans and animals blend into each other so often in the stories. At their core, this is what the sagas are also trying to convey: the unity of existence. It's what nature is expressing too, with every pulse of its infinite, interconnected variety.

This whole notion is radically different from our current, legal understanding of land and also from the

Christian model of an inanimate earth on which a male
deity created animals and man for his own glory or as a
proving ground for entry to Heaven. The Church and the
judiciary try to separate everything so that they can be
recategorised under their specific rule of God or law, but
it's just not how nature works. It's vital that we bear this
in mind, especially in this era of environmental strain.
Our bodies and minds are part of a complex biofeedback
loop with the soil and water that links us to all creation.
And so much of recent scientific discovery seems to be
pointing to the truth that the earth is alive and that its
health can be gauged by the state of its tissues and organs
– the wetlands, rivers, forests and soil. Simply put, all life
is unified and interconnected. We cannot survive beyond
our surroundings. We are part of the land, and the land
wishes to communicate with us.

CONCLUSIONS

What should be clear from these diverse explorations is that our people were once rooted to a profound degree in the autonomy of the land and the energies that arose from it. As long as we had a connection with this world and the world beyond, and the knowledge of how these realms reacted to each other, we had power. We understood that there were different realities that could be accessed, or at least imagined, if necessary, and this made us strong.

In recent years we have become dissociated from this knowledge and the latent appreciation that our ancestors had of the natural world and the cycles through which it turns, as well as the realms beyond, in both the cosmos and the Otherworld. So much has been lost, but it's not through any fault of our own. Those who sought to colonise us realised it was vital that we be severed from this. Each successive group who came to subjugate us saw it as a priority to disconnect us from our power. All had an agenda to promulgate and an authoritarian regime to enforce. They made sure to close down the sacred areas or supersede them with centres of their own on top of the original sites or nearby.

So successful were they at disconnecting us from our power points that we now happily build a motorway through the royal site at Tara, and ignore sites like the Hill of Uisneach, Rathcroghan and Lough Gur. We have forgotten where our power lies and now sneer at and denigrate these inland and less dramatically picturesque areas that were once our *axis mundi* – the cosmic frontier where the sacred and the physical meet.

It's about time we cast off our blinkers and remember how this island has always been a vibrant, buoyant, spiritually nourishing place, activated by a belief in animism, which recognises that nature is infused with an illuminating life force that imbues it with sanctity. We are descendants of the seers who so frightened and mystified the Romans and Greeks two thousand years ago, and also of the eccentric, spiritually promiscuous monastic missionaries who brought a uniquely nature-focused, land-rooted form of Christianity back to the war-devastated ruins of central Europe a thousand years later, after the Goths, Vandals and Visigoths had wiped out much of civilisation in the Dark Ages.

I've been critical of the censorship that Christianity imposed on the old nature-worshipping beliefs of our people, of how it helped break our connection with the land and the female deities that animated it. They also broke our connection with the concept of planetary alignments within the solar system. Yet it was also the monks who preserved all the prehistoric, pagan lore in oak gall ink on calfskin pages. They were deeply influenced by it, it seems, as Ireland developed a unique form of Celtic Christianity that was infused with aspects of the pre-Christian belief, such as the worshipping of sacred wells and trees and of the few earth deities that lingered, like Brigid.

The monks developed a form of animistic Christianity that they then spread to Europe in the seventh and eighth centuries. These oddball missionaries who wrote poems about the beauty of the blackbird's call, or the white-thorn's berries, or a midland lake at dawn, became beacons of light for a culturally slaughtered Europe. These were the likes of St Feargal from Co. Laois, who went to Salzburg, or St Killian from Cavan, who went to Würzburg, or the many other Irish monks who went to Italy and France to bring light to the darkness.

It's just what we've always done: taken strength, insight and wisdom from a deeply rooted connection with land and spirit and used it as the animating force in our lives. I'm not saying every Irish person was like this, but there have always been poets, seers, monks, healers and wise women who immersed themselves in the land-scape and used their connection to light creative fires in themselves and others. It's just what we do.

The question now, as the feminine energy is rising once again, is whether we as Irish people – and those of other cultures who connect with us – are ready to take back this mantle and begin the process of awakening and reconnecting with our past, with who we are – our land, language and culture. We shouldn't underestimate the power of this land as a force of transformation. The bogs, rivers, mountains and shorelines are more than just preservers of old myths, bones and memories. They are energy banks and time sponges, and what is held within them seeks release.

ACKNOWLEDGEMENTS

To my parents, Cróine and Michael, for all the expeditions they organised to historical sites, forested demesnes, mountain passes, island sanctuaries and archaeological digs that sparked in me a curiosity about the landscape and culture of this island. Their active involvement with the Irish Georgian Society and the Friends of the National Collection of Ireland taught me to be constantly scanning the natural and built environment, and learning the stories of my locality.

Experiencing my father's encyclopaedic knowledge of the local history of almost every square inch of Ireland brought home to me the phenomenal richness of our cultural legacy, and watching my mother's relentless campaigns in the 1970s to preserve landmark buildings, such as Tailors' Hall in the Liberties of Dublin and Damer House in Roscrea, made clear to me the importance of fighting to preserve our heritage, just as her mother, Sighle Humphreys and grand-uncle, The O'Rahilly, had fought to gain Ireland's independence.

It was in 1978, when my whole family joined the battle to prevent the destruction of Viking Dublin at Wood Quay, that I truly understood the importance of our cultural heritage. Just as Sighle had been instrumental in supporting the IRA during the War of Independence in the 1920s, my siblings and I actively supported the brave volunteers who camped in front of bulldozers to prevent the destruction of our archaeological inheritance.

To Dr Peter Harbison, for permitting me, as a gormless teenager in the 1980s, to tag along as he walked the hills of the Dingle Peninsula developing his theory of Early Christian and medieval pilgrimage in Ireland. I learnt from him how to feel my way into a landscape and to strip away a thousand years in order to see how the land looked long ago. Thanks to Peter for his early edits of this book and for offering such valuable insights and advice.

To Conor Newman of NUIG, who has been such a great supporter and who has pointed me towards invaluable sources and resources that have enriched this book.

To my lecturers at University College Dublin who so inspired me in the early 1990s, particularly Professor Francis J. Byrne and Dr Charlie Doherty of the Early Irish History department, and Professor Howard Clarke, who brought medieval Dublin alive for me.

To Professor Daithí Ó hÓgáin of the Folklore Department of UCD, who took me under his wing, despite the fact that I wasn't even enrolled in any of his courses.

To my relations from North Kerry: Fr. F.X. Martin, professor of Medieval History; T.F. O'Rahilly, professor of Celtic Languages; and Cecile O'Rahilly, professor of Celtic Studies, who established a precedent for the rigour, excellence and eloquence needed to say something new in the field of Early Irish History.

To my brother Ruán for offering his insights into the Famine chapters and to the many scholars who have patiently taken the time to explain their field of expertise or shared their research with me: Dr Roseanne Schot, Ciara Henderson, Daniel Curley, Mike McCarthy, Donnchadh Ó Baoill, Rossa Ó Snodaigh, Cathal Ó Baoill and Anthony Murphy, curator of the great archive mythicalireland.com. I apologise if my limited abilities have failed to capture the excellence of their research and insights.

To Steve Doogan, whose cover design and illustrations have done so much to lift my three books with Gill Books to a whole other level.

To Michael Keegan-Dolan, who first challenged me to have the courage to publish my vision for the Irish language in *Thirty-Two Words For Field*, without which this book would not exist.

To Marianne Gunn O'Connor, my literary agent, who has steered me safely through the world of writing for 15 years, and to Jessica Woollard, who is now taking over the baton.

And most of all, to Aisling Rogerson, who sparked this entire work by her wish to gift her baker at the Fumbally Café a book about the sacredness of the Irish landscape. She challenged me to find such a book, and I failed the challenge. Two years later, these pages are my humble offering.

INDEX